Computers, Cockroaches, and Ecosystems: Understanding Learning through Metaphor

Computers, Cockroaches, and Ecosystems: Understanding Learning through Metaphor

Kevin J. Pugh

INFORMATION AGE PUBLISHING, INC.
Charlotte, NC • www.infoagepub.com

Library of Congress Cataloging-in-Publication Data

Paperback: 9781681237763
Hardcover: 9781681237770
eBook: 9781681237787

CONTENTS

PART 3

CONSTRUCTIVISM

PART 4

SOCIOCULTURALISM

PART 5

THE PURPOSE OF LEARNING

CHAPTER 1

THE LEARNING AGE

> When we started to work on the atomic bomb project at Los Alamos, every-thing was in such a hurry that it wasn't really ready. All the secrets of the projects—everything about the atomic bomb—were kept in filing cabinets which, if they had locks at all, were locked with padlocks which had maybe three pins: they were as easy as pie to open.
>
> —*Feynman, 1985, p. 138*

That's legendary physicist Richard Feynman on the Manhattan Project, where he displayed his knack for tinkering and making mischief, as well as his tenacity for learning.

Feynman was an obvious recruit for the Manhattan Project, which developed the first nuclear weapons. However, he quickly wreaked havoc by breaking into locked filing cabinets just to show how easy it was. The government soon installed new filing cabinets with built-in combination locks—the spinning kind you probably had on your high school locker. Feynman was thrilled, "These new filing cabinets were an immediate challenge, naturally. I love puzzles. One guy tries to make something to keep another guy out; there must be a way to beat it!" (p. 139).

Feynman took apart his own file cabinet, studied the mechanics, and began figuring out how to crack the combination. He did this for a year and half, and

Computers, Cockroaches, and Ecosystems: Understanding Learning Through Metaphor,
pages 1–9.
Copyright © 2017 by Information Age Publishing

learned a few things. First, the combination did not have to be exact. He could be off by two numbers in either direction. Thus, a 100-number dial could be reduced to 20 numbers (0, 5, 10, …). Second, if the file cabinet was open and the dial undisturbed, he could fairly easily get the last two numbers of a three-number combination by noting the actions of the locking bolt as he turned the dial by fives in one direction and then the other. After figuring this out, he spent hours practicing until he could get the last two numbers of a combination while barely looking at the dial.

He then went about picking off the last two numbers of his colleagues' combination locks. When anyone had a file cabinet open, Feynman would causally lean against it, fiddle with the dial in a seemingly meaningless way, and get the last two numbers. Breaking into a file cabinet now became easy. All he had to do was try each of the 20 possible first numbers with the last two numbers, which he had written down and filed away.

He once used this technique to crack a colonel's safe. Feynman thought it was a valuable security demonstration, but the colonel was not amused.

After the war, Feynman returned to Los Alamos to complete a report. He needed papers from a locked file cabinet in colleague Freddy de Hoffman's office. The file cabinet was one in a set of nine holding copies of the atom bomb secrets, but that did not stop Feynman from trying to crack the lock.

Lacking the last two numbers of this lock combination, he tried a different approach. First, he searched the secretary's desk for written numbers and found pi scribbled to six digits. Feynman tried using pi in varying sequences but with no success. However, he figured de Hoffman was likely to use another mathematical constant for a combination. Therefore, he went back to the file cabinets and tried another famous number[1]. Not only did the first file cabinet open, but so did the next two. They all had the same combination!

Later that day, Feynman followed de Hoffman into his office. De Hoffman opened a file cabinet and found this message in red crayon on a bright yellow note: "When the combinations are all the same, one is no harder to open than the other—Same Guy." De Hoffman turned white and looked sick. He opened a second cabinet and found a second note, "This one is no harder to open than the other one—Wise Guy." De Hoffman started shaking. These file cabinets held secrets to the *atom bomb*. He opened a third file cabinet and found, "I borrowed document no. LA4312—Feynman the safecracker."

When I first read Feynman's (1985) collection of autobiographical stories, I was struck by his passion for learning. Teaching himself how to crack locks is but one story (although one of my favorites) of putting his mind to something and pursuing it until he figured it out. He also became a successful percussionist and sketch artist. Other stories range from learning to fix radios as a child to di-

---

[1] 2.718… or e which is the base of the natural logarithm.

agnosing the cause of the Challenger disaster. Not bad for a Nobel Prize-winning quantum physicist.

The world needs more Richard Feynmans. Or, perhaps more accurately, we all need a bit more Feynman in us. The world is changing at breakneck speed. Information is exploding, cultures are colliding, and whole industries are emerging, transforming and dissolving. People say we are in the knowledge age or information age, but it really should be called the learning age. To learn is our great challenge and our great opportunity.

Surprisingly, most people have relatively little formal knowledge about the nature of learning. I am often impressed by the intuitive knowledge about learning others gain through experience. However, in terms of formal principles, most people are only familiar with broad theories about various learning styles: audio, visual, kinesthetic; left brain, right brain; multiple intelligences, and so on. These theories are popular with the general public, but learning experts paint a very different picture.

Most learning experts consider learning styles and so called "brain-based" explanations for learning to be fringe or superficial ideas about learning without much empirical support (for critiques, see Furnham, 2012; Waterhouse, 2006). David Bergin, a past president of the educational psychology division of the American Psychological Association, told me, "Learning styles are intuitively appealing, but there is little or no evidence that claiming to measure someone's learning style and then attempting to teach to that learning style improves learning" (personal communication, April 28, 2014).

The goal of this book is to popularize the core principles of learning valued by learning experts. The book is written for anyone with an interest in learning—including students, parents, counselors and military or business trainers. However, it is particularly designed for teachers, who are at the forefront of the learning challenge. Teachers must foster learning, but also prepare individuals for this learning age. Understanding the true nature of learning is critical to their success, and to our success as a learning society. Unfortunately, even teachers do not always thoroughly understand the core learning principles. My own disastrous student teaching experience is a good example.

Over two decades ago, I was a green student teacher trying to teach high school psychology. The supervising teacher and I did not exactly have the same view of education. His view was traditional. Students sat in their desks and took notes while he lectured and pointed to important information in the textbook. My view was...well, fuzzy. And that was a problem.

I had a vague sense that the learning in this classroom was not very effective, and I had an even vaguer sense of how I could accomplish learning that is more effective. In fact, "vague" is an understatement because I had virtually no scientific knowledge of the nature of learning. In my teacher education program, I learned about teaching strategies, lesson planning, classroom management, and so on. Somehow, though, I failed to learn anything about the learning process.

Consequently, when it was my turn to teach, I began pursuing this goal of effective learning that I knew nothing about. One day, I decided that students would learn psychology if they did a psychological experiment. This may have been a reasonable idea, but I could not define or support the real learning goal. Consequently, students were running around doing who knows what. I would move around the room, talk to groups, and try to "support their learning."

My supervising teacher would sit in the back of the room, watching in horror as his well-structured class dissolved into chaos. Once a break came, he would lead me into his office, take some deep breaths, sigh, and ask, "What were you trying to do out there?"

This is when my lack of knowledge of learning really hurt me. I had no way of articulating the project or my goal. I would fumble around and say things like, "I…I was trying to get them to design experiments."

"Why?"

"Well…I thought they might learn something by doing their own experiment."

"Learn what? What was your objective? What was the content you were trying to cover?"

"I…I wasn't thinking about particular content. I was just thinking they would like learn…learn about…learn something."

"Two students were standing on top of their desks."

"I know…I think it might have had something to do with their experiment…maybe."

"Other students were chasing each other around the classroom."

"Um…"

[sigh] "I didn't see much learning going on out there."

I could not dispute this point, but I also thought to myself, "*Yeah, but I don't know that there is much learning going on when you have them copy notes either. Isn't learning something more?*" I did not verbalize these thoughts (I was not that dumb), and I could not have verbalized anything intelligent anyway. I really did not have much depth of thought beyond "learning is something more."

Today, I could articulate how copying notes was unlikely to change existing misconceptions (chapter 6), create the kind of knowledge structures important to enduring memory (chapter 4), support the application of learning in real-world contexts (chapter 8), or help students experience the relevance of learning in everyday life (chapters 9 and 10). I could also critique problems with my own approach, such as overloading students' capacity to process new information (chapter 3). However, as a flailing student teacher, all I could say is learning must be something more. Therefore, I continued to experiment with teaching that might yield "something more," and my supervising teacher continued to be baffled by my incompetence. Eventually, I completed my time, much to his relief.

In subsequent years, I have studied learning and taught others about learning, and I have reached a few conclusions.

- Learning is not just a byproduct of innate brilliance. Richard Feynman certainly was brilliant, but this does not adequately explain his learning success. As you will see in chapter 7, innate intelligence as measured by IQ counts for surprisingly little in terms of learning success. Everyone has the potential to learn. By understanding the nature of learning, we can achieve our potential and foster potential in others.
- Learning is far more diverse and complex that we typically realize. There are many different learning processes related to many different learning outcomes. To maximize our learning potential and that of others, we need to understand these processes.
- There are well-developed learning theories explaining these learning processes.
- These learning theories can best be understood through their key metaphors. At the heart of each learning theory is a metaphor or two that captures the essence of the theory. If you can understand the metaphors, you can understand the theories. This book is all about those metaphors.

I address metaphors central to five major learning perspectives: behaviorism, cognitivism, constructivism, socioculturalism, and Dewey's philosophy of education. Each chapter presents a different metaphor and unpacks the meaning of the metaphor through illustrative stories and real-world accounts. I also discuss implications for learning and teaching of each metaphor. However, a comprehensive review of implications is not my intent. This is not another "how to" book telling teachers, parents, or students all the things they should do. Rather, I hope to spark musings about the meaning and ramifications of each core metaphor. Finally, some metaphors raise existential questions about the nature of reality or the reality of an individual mind. I present these questions for you to contemplate, without getting too philosophical.

In sum, that's how each chapter works. Here is a roadmap of those chapters.

Chapter 2 presents a key behaviorist metaphor: *learning as natural selection*. Behaviorism grew out of an attempt to make psychology a true science by focusing exclusively on that which is observable and measurable, i.e. behavior. Thus, the study of learning became a study of linkages between behavior and environment. It was only a small step from Darwin's thesis of environment selecting traits in organisms to the behaviorist thesis of environment selecting behaviors in humans.

B. F. Skinner best championed the learning as natural selection perspective. In this view, learning is a process of generating a variety of responses and having some selected by the environment as others go extinct. We are who we are because we have been selected to be that way. Students are who they are because we select them to be that way. Unfortunately, we often select behaviors we do *not* want while failing to select the behaviors we *do* want. This perspective suggests we have a real power to shape behavior and efficiently promote learning. However, it also raises a rather troubling question about the nature of free will. Are we anything more than a set of selected responses?

Over time, researchers concluded that an exclusive focus on observable behavior neglected an important part of learning—the mind! A "cognitive revolution" occurred as researchers began to investigate the secret workings of this all-important organ. The Information Processing Model of memory emerged from this work and chapters 3 and 4 cover metaphors central to this model.

In chapter 3, I explore the computer as a foundational metaphor for conceptualizing the mind. Indeed, early work in computing technology helped jumpstart the cognitive revolution by providing researchers with an information processing system that could be used to model how the mind processes information. Parallels were drawn in terms how information is encoded, processed, stored, and retrieved, resulting in the Information Processing Model of memory.

I discuss these parallels and their implications for learning, with a particular emphasis on limits in our processing capacity. You might say our CPU is limited compared to our storage capacity. That is, we have a capacity to store vast amounts of information, but we can only process a limited amount at any one time in our working memory. Cognitive researchers refer to this as a cognitive load issue. This issue is relevant for understanding everything from certain cases of autism to the learning differences of novices versus experts.

Chapter 4 focuses on the nature of our storage system (i.e., long-term memory) in the Information Processing model. While the capacity of our storage system is vast, we are horrifyingly bad at using it. Think about all the time and effort you spent acquiring information in school. Out of all that information, how much did you retain? How much can you recall? There is a reason "Are You Smarter than a Fifth Grader?" is such a popular TV show. We forgot everything we learned in fifth grade!

Understanding the nature of our storage system can help us understand why we forget so much, and how we can be more efficient. Two network metaphors can help us understand our long-term storage system. One is the *Internet as knowledge network* metaphor. Understanding long-term memory as a non-linear, linked structure like the Internet explains why some information is easily accessed and other information is not. The second metaphor is the *picture as patterned network*. Pictures represent a pattern of information coming together to create a whole. It turns out such patterns are incredibly important to retaining and accessing information in long-term memory. In chapter 4, I discuss the implications of these metaphors and use them to explain both our memory failures and the incredible feats of memory savants.

Although the computer is a powerful metaphor for the mind's information processing systems, the mind is decidedly *not* like a computer in important ways. Most importantly, the mind is constructive in a way that computers are not. Constructivist learning theories focus on this difference and are the subject of chapters 5 and 6.

Chapter 5 suggests what a computer would be like if it actually functioned like the mind (hint: it would drive you crazy). The chapter illustrates how we construct meaning based on existing ideas, and how we reconstruct rather than recall memories. These seemingly simple principles have radical implications for understanding learning. For instance, after the O. J. Simpson verdict, many were stunned at the different perceptions of guilt between whites and blacks. We all saw the same evidence, right? Not really. The meaning we make of the evidence is dependent on our existing ideas and experiences. We do not see the world in a pure way. We construct a vision of it through the lens of our existing ideas.

Constructivism is also about how we reconstruct memory by recalling memory traces. This is why eyewitness testimonies can be unreliable, and why college students come up with answers like "Joan of Ark was famous as Noah's wife" (Henricksson, 2001). On an existential level, these principles of constructivism raise questions about the nature of reality. Does an objective reality exist? Can we be certain about anything, even our own memories?

Chapter 6 addresses the essential metaphor of constructivism: *mind as ecosystem*. Jean Piaget, often considered the father of constructivism, viewed the mind as an interconnected and dynamic system of ideas reflective of an ecosystem. In this view, the learning of new ideas can be compared to the introduction of new species into an ecosystem.

The mind as ecosystem metaphor is particularly useful for understanding changes in our core beliefs, or lack of change, as is so often the case. It helps us understand why even Harvard graduates can maintain misconceptions they held in fifth grade, why it took 1,500 years to overcome the idea that the earth was the center of the universe, and why we tend to "bend the map," that is, try to make reality fit our preconceptions. It also helps us understand the requirements for genuine change, and how to support such change. Further, this metaphor raises questions about the role of prior knowledge in learning and whether some ideas have greater potential than others to be "invasive species."

The cognitive and constructivists metaphors yield much insight into the nature of the individual mind as a learning object. However, they are largely silent on the social and cultural nature of learning and how both dimensions contribute to the development of the mind. Chapters 7 and 8 address a new set of metaphors that account for social and cultural factors. These metaphors are central to sociocultural and situated learning theories.

Chapter 7 focuses on Vygotsky's *mind as cultural tools* metaphor. Vygotsky was a founder of the sociocultural learning perspective. He argued that cultures create mental tools that mediate mental activity just as physical tools (e.g., shovels) mediate physical activity. Learning is largely a process of internalizing the mental tools of our culture. In fact, mental tools are so important that the mind largely comes into being through the internalization of mental tools. This point is illustrated poignantly through the case of Ildefonso—a man who did not acquire language, the mother of all mental tools, until adulthood. In many ways, Ildefonso's mind came into being through the acquisition of language.

The mind as cultural tools metaphor challenges a number of common assumptions about the mind and learning. For instance, most of us take credit for our own intelligence, and we believe innate intelligence is important to success in life. But what if these assumptions are false? What if our intelligence comes from the mental tools of our culture and such tools are far more important than any innate intelligence? These questions and other implications are addressed in chapter 7.

Chapter 8 addresses the competing metaphors of *knowledge as cockroach versus knowledge as panda bear*. The cognitive and constructivist learning perspectives compare knowledge to the adaptable and resilient cockroach, because it can apply across many different contexts—at least if learned in the correct way. Situated learning theories tend to compare knowledge to the climate- and bamboo-dependent "panda bear," in the sense that it is tied to or "situated" within particular contexts. Instead of focusing on the individual mind, the situative perspective focuses on the context and how the characteristics of that context (particularly social and cultural characteristics) either support or inhibit learning. For example, adolescent learning can often only be fully understood in the context of peer groups and the communities surrounding these peer groups.

The various knowledge metaphors offer various implications for the transfer of learning across contexts. The knowledge as cockroach metaphor leads to a focus on creating highly flexible and adaptive knowledge structures. Cognitive learning theories yield insight into how to create such structures. The knowledge as panda bear metaphor leads to a focus on aligning contexts; that is, making the learning and application contexts as similar as possible. The situative perspective yields insight into how to make such alignment happen.

The final two chapters explore metaphors about the *purpose* of learning. These chapters draw on the philosophy of John Dewey, arguably America's most important educational scholar and philosopher.

Dewey conveyed his vision of the purpose of learning through the metaphor of *learning as the journey versus the map*. Just as a map is a guide for having a journey, so the school curriculum primarily should function as a guide for having a learning journey. In chapter 9, I discuss what it means to "have the journey" and provide examples of such journeys, ranging from boy scout adventures to the experiences of The Freedom Writers.

Dewey also developed a parallel theory of art, and chapter 10 focuses on the *learning as art* metaphor. Art, according to Dewey, can transform our everyday experience. For example, Pop Art taught us to see the beauty in ordinary, everyday objects and events. Likewise, curricular ideas can transform the way we see and experience the everyday world. I provide examples of such transformative learning and discuss some of the conditions needed for transformative learning such as a willingness to "surrender" to the learning experience. I also discuss lessons we can learn from art, such as the problem with "classic status" and ways we can artistically craft the content.

We are in the age of learning. Yet the core principles of learning are not common knowledge. This is a problem. On the bright side, these core principles are accessible; their essence can be readily understood through their central metaphors. So, without further ado, onto the metaphors.

REFERENCES

Feynman, R. P. (1985). *"Surely you're joking, Mr. Feynman!": Adventures of a curious character*. New York, NY: Quality Paperback Book Club.

Furnham, A. (2012). Learning styles and approaches to learning. In K. R. Harris, S. Graham, & T. Urdan (Eds.), *APA educational psychology handbook, Vol. 2: Individual differences and cultural and contextual factors* (pp. 59–81). Washington, DC: American Psychological Association. doi:10.1037/13274-003

Henriksson, A. (2001). *Non campus mentis: World history according to college students.* New York: Workman.

Waterhouse, L. (2006). Multiple intelligences, the Mozart effect, and emotional intelligence: A critical review. *Educational Psychologist, 41*, 207–225. doi:10.1207/s15326985ep4104_1

PART 1

BEHAVIORISM

In the early 20th century, Behaviorism emerged in response to criticisms of psychology. Psychology was labeled a pseudoscience because its theories could not be falsified. For example, Freud proposed that male children ages 3 to 6 have an Oedipus complex that drives unconscious urges to kill their fathers and marry their mothers. Today that seems like a crazy idea, but how could you ever prove it false?

Behaviorists chose to study psychology scientifically by focusing exclusively on what was observable and measurable, namely, behavior. Learning was defined in terms of observable behavioral outcomes and the mind was considered a "black box" that could not be observed or studied scientifically. Instead, behaviorist researchers focused their efforts on identifying associations between behaviors and things happening in the environment.

Inevitably, some researchers, most notably B. F. Skinner, began drawing on Darwin's ideas to explain the origin and evolution of behavior (Skinner, 1984a; 1984b). If species originated and evolved through a process of selection by the environment, could not the same be said of behaviors? Chapter 2 addresses this idea.

CHAPTER 2

LEARNING AS NATURAL SELECTION

To understand the *learning as natural selection* metaphor, we first need to understand natural section. One of the best illustrations of natural[1] selection is the
change that took place in the peppered moth population near London, England,
during the industrial revolution. Prior to the industrial revolution, nearly all the
peppered moths in the area were light-colored, with a small percentage being
dark-colored. However, by the mid–19th century, nearly all were dark-colored.
Why?

A high school biology teacher asked his students this question while I observed
his class as part of a research study. Answers included, "The moths got sooty,"
"They hid in the shadows," "They migrated," "They wanted to adapt," and "They
got tan" (Pugh, Linnenbrink-Garcia, Koskey, Stewart, & Manzey, 2010, p. 291).
As much as I like the image of moths hanging out in sunglasses getting a tan, that
was not the answer. Neither is it true that the moths hid in the shadows, migrated,
or got sooty. So what did happen? The answer has to do with the trees.

---

[1] Humans affected the environment in this example, so "natural" in this case includes humans as part
of nature.

Computers, Cockroaches, and Ecosystems: Understanding Learning through Metaphor,
pages 13–23.

Prior to the industrial revolution, the trees had light-colored bark and lichen. The light-colored moths blended in perfectly with this background, and the dark-colored moths stood out like a sore thumb. Consequently, the dark-colored moths were far more likely to be spotted and eaten by birds, so few survived. However, during the industrial revolution, the trees became blanketed by soot, and much of the lichen died. Now the dark-colored moths blended into the background, and the light-colored moths stood out.

The term "survival of the fittest" means organisms with traits that fit the environment are more likely to survive, reproduce, and sustain or expand the population. Organisms with traits that do not fit the environment are more likely to die off. When the trees were light, the light-colored moths better fit the environment, so they flourished. But when the trees became darkened, the dark-colored moths became more fit for survival.

It is vital to remember that the change in the peppered moth population had nothing to do with the moths' intentions. The moths had no control over the change. They simply continued to live and reproduce, and a change in the environment caused a change in the population. In natural selection, the environment selects traits in a population. Individuals cannot adapt or change their own traits.[2]

MAKING SENSE OF THE METAPHOR.

People do strange things. In addition to cracking locks while working on the Manhattan project, Richard Feynman played bongo drums alone in the mountains. Nikola Tesla, another brilliant scientist, obsessed over the number three and did things like walk around a building three times before entering. Michael Jordan wore an old pair of college shorts under his Chicago Bulls shorts because he thought they brought him luck. On days off, Babe Ruth wore women's silk stockings for the same reason. Steve Jobs had to work the night shift during his time at Atari because he did not bathe. Britney Spears shaved her head. Tom Cruise jumped up and down on Oprah's couch. Kim Kardashian does Kim Kardashian stuff. And so on.

We tend to believe that people do bizarre things because they are nuts. B. F. Skinner disagreed. He would say it has nothing to do with the person and everything to do with the environment. The behaviors we manifest are *selected for* by the environment (Skinner, 1965).

In Skinner's view, behaviors are like traits. Individuals display a variety of behaviors just as a population of organisms displays a variety of traits. Some of these behaviors are selected for and these "fit" behaviors survive, while others die off. Thus, your actions, habits, and personality—everything that makes you *you*—are the end result of a long history of selection by the environment. *You are who you are because you have been selected to be that way.*

---

[2] Although modern research suggests modification to this classic Darwinian view.

Such selection takes place by means of reinforcement and punishment. Reinforcement is any positive consequence, and punishment is any negative consequence. These consequences can be tangible, such as receiving a gold star or losing a privilege, or intangible, such as receiving praise or criticism. Skinner's *operant conditioning* principle states that reinforced behaviors are strengthened and likely repeated. Punished behaviors are weakened and probably will not be repeated (Skinner, 1965). Behaviors that are neither reinforced nor punished will also go extinct over time. Reinforcement is needed to sustain a behavior.

Skinner particularly encouraged shaping behavior through active reinforcement. In fact, he believed punishment was often unnecessary because proactive and systematic reinforcement of desirable behavior typically eliminates the need to punish undesirable behavior. Most of us focus our (ineffective) efforts toward punishment when reinforcement is the better option.

As an example of behavior becoming selected and shaped through reinforcement, consider the following story shared by Skinner (1986). One day, two students approached him with a question. They liked to decorate with modern art but their new roommate preferred banners and sports trophies. Could they condition him to appreciate modern art? Skinner, of course, believed they could and so they did. Here is how it went down:

> They began by paying little or no attention to him unless he asked about their paintings and sculptures. They gave a party and bribed a young woman to ask the roommate about these art objects, and to hang on his every word. ... They went [with him to the Boston Museum of Fine Arts], and when they saw him looking at a picture that he seemed especially to like, they dropped a $5 bill on the floor. He looked down and found the bill. (Skinner, 1986, p. 109)

Within the next month, the roommate bought his first modern art painting. Around 30 years later, one of the students ran into the roommate at, wait for it, the Museum of Modern Art.

In this story (which, I admit, cracks me up and disturbs me at the same time), positive attention and money were systematically presented as consequences for behaviors associated with an attraction to modern art. Hence, these behaviors were reinforced and selected for by the environment.

Skinner proposed that all types of learning occurred through this same process, and academic learning was no exception. We learn writing, math, science, history, and so on by being reinforced for making correct responses.

Finally, for something to be an effective reinforcer, two conditions must be met. First, that something—referred to as a stimulus—has to be *contingent* on the behavior. That is, the stimulus must occur in response to the behavior, such that the individual either consciously or unconsciously associates the stimulus with the behavior. This usually means the stimulus needs to immediately follow the behavior. The sitcom "The Big Bang Theory" offers a politically incorrect example. In the show, Sheldon the awkward scientist is trying to "reform" his loud and gregarious neighbor, Penny. He gives her a piece of chocolate every time she performs a behavior he deems appropriate, such as zipping her lips, taking a phone call outside, and speaking in a lower voice. Because the chocolate is given immediately after the desired behavior, a contingency is established and Penny conforms to Sheldon's "training" even though she is not aware of what is going on.

Too often, reinforcements are not immediate and a contingency is not established. For instance, Skinner was critical of most grading systems and similar rewards in school because they are not immediate and they are too loosely tied to specific behaviors.

Second, the stimulus has to be something desirable to the individual. This is not as simple as it sounds. We do not all have the same likes and desires. For many people, including one of my daughters, attention is largely undesirable. She hates it. For others, any form of attention, even negative attention, is desirable. This variation can explain many strange behaviors. As I will describe shortly, it is also a main reason we unintentionally reinforce unwanted behaviors in others.

IMPLICATIONS

We Have the Power and Responsibility to Shape Effective Learning Environments.

"These students just don't care. It's impossible to teach them." "Braydon is such a troublemaker. He drives me crazy." "Joline is so lazy. She never does her work." In the behaviorist perspective, these statements have no validity. Blaming the students is just a way of dodging responsibility for the environment. After all, the environment determines behavior.

If students are misbehaving or not engaging, then the problem is with the reinforcement structure. Teachers, parents, and administrators need to be thoughtful about creating structured environments that reinforce appropriate behaviors. One formal approach to doing this is Applied Behavioral Analysis (ABA). ABA consists of these five steps:

1. **Identify the inappropriate and target (i.e., the desired) behaviors in observable, measurable terms.** Behaviors need to be defined concretely, so teachers can track their frequency and analyze the precursors and consequences (step 2). For instance, "off-task behavior" is too vague. For ABA, the teacher needs to define off-task behavior in terms of concrete behaviors, such as "texting during class."

2. **Identify the environmental causes of the inappropriate behavior.** If a behavior is occurring, something must be reinforcing the behavior. This is a central tenet of Skinner's operant conditioning theory. Hence, the first step toward eliminating inappropriate behavior is to find out how the environment is reinforcing it. To do so, observe and record the pre-

cursors and consequences of a behavior. For example, keep a log (to the degree possible) of what happens immediately before the display of an inappropriate behavior (precursors) and what happens immediately afterward (consequences). The precursors may be cues that prompt the behavior and the consequences are likely to be the reinforcers that sustain the behavior. For example, through careful observation, a teacher may realize that, each time Joe makes an inappropriate comment in class, his friends smirk or start nodding. Such actions are likely reinforcing Joe's inappropriate comments. Remember, reinforcers are dependent on what the student finds desirable. So if the consistent consequence of a student's inappropriate behavior is the teacher "punishing" the student by criticizing him or her, it may be that the student finds such criticism desirable (hey, at least it is some form of attention) and the criticism is actually reinforcing the behavior.

3. **Develop an intervention plan.** Once the likely cause has been identified, an intervention plan should be developed, with three components.

   a. *A plan for changing the setting events.* Setting events are conditions in the environment that make a certain behavior more or less likely. They are not reinforcers or punishers, but are simply features of the environment. For example, if I want to go on a healthy diet, then I might change the food I have lying around the house. If I keep seeing a bunch of junk food, I will struggle to stick to my diet.

   b. *A plan to eliminate reinforcement of the problem behavior.* Step two identifies likely reinforcers of the inappropriate behavior. Now the teacher designs a systematic plan for eliminating these reinforcers. However, keep in mind that it might be difficult to fully eliminate existing reinforcers.

   c. *A plan to shape the target behavior.* This is the crux of ABA. Just as Skinner's students changed the behavior of their roommate by systematically reinforcing target behaviors, so teachers can change behavior through systematic reinforcement. In some cases, this can be more informal such as simply making a concerted effort to praise or acknowledge the target behavior (assuming the student finds such praise or acknowledgement desirable). In other cases, it can involve a more formal system, such as a token economy. In a token economy, which is used more commonly with younger or special needs individuals, students are given tokens regularly for appropriate responses (e.g., raising a hand before speaking; working on worksheet for five minutes). These tokens can then be exchanged for prizes.

4. **Monitor the behavior and revise the intervention as needed.** After implementing the plan, the teacher continues to monitor the frequency of

the inappropriate and target behaviors. If progress is being made, great. If not, the teacher works on revising the implementation plan.

5. **Fade out the intervention.** If possible, try to transition from overt and more artificial external reinforcers to more natural or internal reinforcers. For example, a teacher may help a student recognize feelings of satisfaction that come from achieving success, and the connection between the target behavior and achieving success. Over time, success becomes the reinforcer, and the teacher fades out the formal reward system.

ABA can be very effective at changing behavior. However, it is not without its critics. For one, many teachers do not feel they have time for such an involved system. Practically speaking, it makes more sense to use ABA when other less time-consuming strategies are not working. In addition, many people do not fully accept the foundational claim that environment *determines* behavior. Consequently, they believe ABA is incomplete because it does teach students to take responsibility for their own behavior.

Personally, I agree it is important for students to take responsibility for their behavior and learning. However, I also believe we often unfairly blame students and neglect our own obligation to create an environment that best supports and encourages effective learning.

Be Careful What You Reinforce.

Even though we have the power to shape desirable behavior, we often shape undesirable behavior instead. Take this parenting scenario as an example. Just as you finally get a chance to relax and read a magazine, you hear the baby wake from her nap. You think, "Hmm, maybe she'll go back to sleep" and start glancing through the magazine. The baby does not go back to sleep but begins to cry softly. You think, "That was a short nap. She should really go back to sleep. Please go back to sleep" and begin reading an article that caught your eye. Soon the baby is crying in earnest and you say to yourself, "OK, OK, I'm coming" while you quickly try to finish the article. The crying escalates, so finally you drop the magazine, rush in, pick up the baby, and give her lots of love. What have you just done? You just reinforced the baby for crying really loud for a really long time! (If you are a parent, you have done this. You can admit it.)

In education, we often make the same mistake of unintentionally reinforcing undesirable behavior—or failing to reinforce desirable behavior. When one of my daughters was in kindergarten, she told us she did not want to go to school anymore. What? She used to love school. What happened? We found out the teacher decided to put the rowdy kids in the front of the class where she could keep an eye on them, and she sent the well-behaved kids to the back. My daughter was among those sent to be back, and now she felt she was always being ignored. So I gave her some advice.

"Sierra, when you have something you want to share, raise your hand really high and wave it about," I told her. "Actually, first jump out of your seat and then wave it around. Or better yet, climb on your seat and wave it around. And do not wait to be called on. Just start shouting out what you want to say. Do this enough, and you'll get sent back to the front of the class again!"

She gave me the stink eye instead of taking the advice.

Sometimes we reinforce undesirable behavior because we do not think about consequences from a student's perspective. For a couple years, a teenager in foster care would spend her weekends with us. When I asked about her school week, our conversations would go something like this.

Me:	So, how was school this week?
Princess	(yes, that is her name): It was OK. Kinda borin' but OK. I went most of the week."
Me:	Only most of the week?
Princess:	[laughing] Yeah, well on Thursday I was late to class, so the teacher, he send me to detention.
Me:	Oh? And how did detention go.
Princess:	I didn't go. I don't mind detention. Like, it's ok. But I wasn't feelin' it, ya know?
Me:	And … how did that work out?
Princess:	They suspend me. [laughs] So, yeah, so Tiff and I … on Friday, Tiff and I goes to the mall and we hang out there and it was so fun cuz we do all this crazy stuff like…

It soon became apparent that the school's punishments were actually rewards for Princess. I tried telling her she could greatly benefit from being the first person in her family to go to college. But, in line with Skinner's theories, what mattered for Princess were the immediate consequences (getting out of class or out of school all together) of past behavior, not the possible future consequences.

We also set up systems that unintentionally reinforce unwanted behaviors. For example, the No Child Left Behind law tied rewards and punishments to the percentage of students achieving proficiency on state standardized reading and math tests. In this system, schools were reinforced for increasing reading and math performance, but not for increasing performance in other subjects. Guess which subjects started getting less and less instructional time? Not only was more time spent on the subjects being tested, but also focus was placed on those skills most frequently assessed on past tests, and time was allocated to learning test-taking skills (Jennings & Bearak, 2014).

In addition, by rewarding or punishing schools based on the percentage of proficient students, NCLB incentivized schools for focusing on students just below the proficiency threshold. Think about it. There is no reward for increasing the learning of those who are already proficient. And there is only a reward for increasing the learning of low-achieving students if they cross the proficiency threshold. In other words, struggling students, unlikely to cross the threshold, are not worth the effort.

Finally, you can increase the percentage of proficient students either by increasing their learning or making the state test easier. The latter is exactly what many states seemed to do. Nearly every state had a higher percentage of students who were proficient on the state test than on the National Assessment of Educational Progress (NAEP), with Mississippi taking the cake. In 2005, that state had the highest percentage of students proficient on the state test and lowest percentage of students proficient on the NAEP (Wallis & Steptoe, 2007).

Response, Reinforce, Repeat

Generations are the time stamps of natural selection. Each generation is an opportunity to select for a particular trait. Thus, fruit flies and other organisms with short lifespans are popular targets of experimentation. In terms of selecting behavior, the equivalents of generations are response-reinforcement cycles. Thus, a way to speed up learning is to speed up the response-reinforcement cycles. This means providing many opportunities to make responses and receive reinforcement.

Skinner (1986) believed he could greatly increase the efficiency of learning with his "programmed instruction." In programmed instruction, an expert designs an extensive sequence of quiz items to lead learners through the content in an orderly and cumulative way. After trying each item, the learner receives immediate feedback on whether the response was correct. Skinner argued that success itself is a reinforcer of behavior. Individuals simply need to know a response was correct for that response to be reinforced. Thus, in programed instruction, learners go through hundreds of response-reinforcement cycles in a relatively short period of time.

Skinner would have appreciated today's computer learning programs, in which students provide answers to questions and receive immediate feedback, often accompanied by stars, points, or happy noises. He also would have been a fan of programs like Direct Instruction (Engelmann & Carnine, 1982), in which students respond in unison to a constant and fast-paced stream of prompts and questions. For example, a reading lesson might proceed as follows:

Teacher:	The sound '*vvv*' is usually spelled 've.' *Cave*. Say it.
Students:	Cave.
Teacher:	What sound is at the end of the word?
Students:	*vvv*
Teacher:	How do you spell it?
Students:	V E
Teacher:	Good.

This sequence might be repeated numerous times with other "ve" words. Throughout the day, students make hundreds of responses, and correct responses are reinforced occasionally by the teacher but mainly by the success of responding in unison with the other students.

Skinner was highly critical of any sort of discovery learning, believing it was a waste of time to have students figure things out on their own. Instead, teachers should provide instruction and reinforce proper responses to the instruction. One of the great debates in education is the struggle between teacher-centered and student-centered education. Skinner clearly favored a teacher-centered model. He believed the teacher should control the learning by determining the content, providing instruction and shaping behavior through reinforcement. Other perspectives, particularly the constructivist perspective (see chapters 5 and 6) provide a counter viewpoint, emphasizing the active role of students in the learning process.

Is Free Will an Illusion?

Most of us accept that behavior is *influenced* by the environment. But *determined*? We are not so comfortable with that idea. Skinner, however, did not shy away from this proposition. In a classic book, *Beyond Freedom and Dignity*, Skinner (1971) argued that free will is an illusion. We only think we are in control of our actions because we are unaware of the full history of reinforcement that determines our responses in any given situation. Just as the peppered moth population was acted upon by the environment and had no choice in the matter, so we are acted upon and have no choice in the matter.

For instance, suppose you are approached by a dog at a park. You reach out and pet the dog. You think you chose to pet the dog. However, Skinner would say your act of petting the dog was inevitable given your history of reinforcement. You were likely reinforced for petting dogs in the past by having them react in positive ways: they nuzzle you, lick you, look at you with those adorable eyes. Others praised you for being a dog lover. Along with a thousand other reinforcements, you were shaped to be someone who would reach out and pet that dog.

The above example likely makes some sense to you, but what about more challenging examples? Take, for instance, the actions of a soldier who voluntarily goes to war and puts his life in danger for the good of others. How do you explain this example or other examples of altruistic behavior in terms of Skinner's ideas? Isn't this soldier choosing a course of action *despite* the possible environmental consequences? Skinner would say no. And, indeed, he would say there is no such thing as altruistic behavior. Our soldier is not serving out of moral fortitude or some selfless motive. Instead, Skinner would argue, the soldier is simply responding to past reinforcements.

Perhaps the soldier grew up in a military family. From a young age, he was praised and rewarded for playing like a soldier, dressing like a soldier, acting like a soldier, and so on. Once he expressed a desire to enroll in the military, he was likely reinforced by peers who told him how awesome he was for joining the military. Maybe his girlfriend told him how much she loved him for choosing to serve his country. Once he joined, society would have continued to reinforce his actions by praising him for his service at sporting events, praying for him in church services, and other such acts. Along the way, he also certainly received a lot of vicarious reinforcement[3]. Think of all the movies he saw in which soldiers were praised for their service, awarded medals, and portrayed as heroes. According to Skinner, this reinforcement history determined his behavior.

Scholars continue to debate whether free will is an illusion. However, today's free will skeptics argue that behavior is determined not just by the environment, but also by our genes (Cave, 2016). We are born with inclinations to act in certain ways. Those inclinations, along with environmental consequences, determine our actions. Interestingly, even though many scholars are convinced free will is an illusion, they are reluctant to publicize this conviction—not for fear of criticism, but for fear of the societal consequences stemming from a belief in determinism. Such consequences include a reduction in honesty, commitment, happiness, creativity, gratitude toward others, and many other positive attributes (e.g., Vohs & Schooler, 2008). Saul Smilansky, a philosophy professor at the University of Haifa, in Israel, stated, "We cannot afford for people to internalize the truth" (quoted in Cave, 2016).

REFERENCES

Bandura, A. (1971). Vicarious and self-reinforcement processes. In R. Glaser (Ed.), *The nature of reinforcement* (pp. 228–278). New York, NY: Academic Press.

Cave, S. (2016). There's no such thing as free will: But we're better off believing it anyway. *The Atlantic.* Retrieved from http://www.theatlantic.com/magazine/archive/2016/06/theres-no-such-thing-as-free-will/480750/

Engelmann, S., & Carnine, D. (1982). *Theory of instruction: Principles and applications.* New York, NY: Irvington Publishing.

Jennings, J. L., & Bearak, J. M. (2014). "Teaching to the test" in the NCLB era: How test predictability affects our understanding of student performance. *Educational Researcher, 43,* 381–389. doi:10.3102/0013189X14554449

Pugh, K. J., Linnenbrink-Garcia, L., Koskey, K. L. K., Stewart, V. C., & Manzey, C. (2010). Teaching for transformative experiences and conceptual change: A case study and evaluation of a high school biology teacher's experience. *Cognition and Instruction, 28,* 273–316. doi:10.1080/07370008.2010.490496

Skinner, B. F. (1965). *Science and human behavior.* New York, NY: The Free Press.

Skinner, B. F. (1971). *Beyond freedom and dignity.* New York, NY: Knopf.

Skinner, B. F. (1984a). Selection by consequences. *Behavioral and Brain Sciences, 7,* 477–481. doi:10.1017/S0140525X0002673X

Skinner, B. F. (1984b). The phylogeny and ontogeny of behavior. *Behavioral and Brain Sciences, 7,* 669–677. doi:10.1017/S0140525X00027990

---

[3] In a series of studies, Bandura (1971) found that our behavior is not only shaped by reinforcement we receive but by reinforcement we see others receive. That is, we are likely to imitate behaviors that we see being reinforced.

Skinner, B. F. (1986). Programmed instruction revisited. *Phi Delta Kappan, 68,* 103–110.

Vohs, K. D., & Schooler, J. W. (2008). The value of believing in free will: Encouraging a belief in determinism increases cheating. *Psychological Science, 19,* 49–54. doi:10.1111/j.1467-9280.2008.02045.x

Wallis, C., & Steptoe, S. (2007). How to fix No Child Left Behind. *Time, May 24,* 14–19.

PART 2

COGNITIVISM

When you are developing theories of learning, there is one major problem with ignoring the mind, as the behaviorist perspective did: the mind has a lot to do with learning! For a more complete understanding of learning, researchers began to study the mind and started to understand its nature as a learning machine. Such research became the basis for the cognitive perspective. The term "cognition" refers to the thinking processes of the mind.

Even though the emergence of the cognitive perspective was termed a "cognitive revolution," the behaviorist perspective was not rejected wholesale. Rather, cognitive researchers built on the scientific strategies pioneered by behaviorists. A metaphor illustrates this point.

The Gods Must Be Crazy, an '80s comedy film, is about a Kalahari bushman who is introduced to modern technology in the form of a Coke bottle thoughtlessly tossed out of a small plane. Now imagine, instead of a Coke bottle, it is a car—maybe this is *Fast and Furious 11: Chaos in the Kalahari*—parachuted out of a plane. Further, imagine the car is discovered by bushmen from two tribes: the behaviorist tribe and the cognitive tribe. Each tribe would explore the nature of the car in a different way.

The behaviorist tribe would explore how the car responds when acted upon. That is, they would identify stimulus-response associations. For example, a button is pushed (stimulus), and the car makes a honking noise (response). The cognitive tribe would take it one step farther. They would *develop models of what was going on in the hidden parts of the car*. They might theorize that when a button is pushed, a sharpened stick is moved forward, poking a goose and provoking an angry honk. Based on this theoretical model, the cognitive tribe could make certain predictions (e.g., if the goose is not given water and food, it will die, and the car will not honk when the button is pushed). Testing whether these predictions came true would provide information on whether the theoretical model was valid or not. In this way, the cognitive tribe could scientifically test ideas about what happens in the hidden parts of the car.

Cognitive researchers similarly develop theoretical models of the hidden processes going on in the mind, make predictions based on these models, and test these predictions. The dominant model used for the mind is that of a computer. Chapter 3 presents this *mind as computer* metaphor and describes the Information Processing model of memory derived from this metaphor. Chapter 4 illuminates the nature of long-term memory (a key component of the Information Processing model) through a *mind as network* metaphor.

CHAPTER 3

MIND AS COMPUTER

Robert Epstein thought he had found love through online dating. He met an attractive brunette living near his California hometown. As an immigrant from Russia, her English was broken, but her messages were warm and a relationship began to develop over several months. There was only one problem. She was not real. She was a chatterbot, a computer program written to mimic the conversation of a real human being. Epstein had been duped[1].

The relationship between computers and humans is fascinating, and we are captivated by the potential of computers to mimic human thinking. In fact, each year there is a competition to see if designers can write a program smart enough to be indistinguishable from a live human—the Turing Test, named after the father of computer science, Alan Turing. Epstein himself, an artificial intelligence expert, served as a judge for one of these competitions. So he was not just some schmuck. He was a brilliant scientist with extensive knowledge of chatterbots. And he was still duped. Makes you think, does it not?

In the '50s, learning researchers became aware of the emerging fields of computer science and artificial intelligence. With these machines, which could mimic certain thinking processes, they saw an opportunity to explore the hidden pro-

---

[1] For an account of this story, see Epstein, R. (2007). From Russia, with love: How I got fooled (and somewhat humiliated) by a computer. *Scientific American Mind, 18*(5), 16–17.

Computers, Cockroaches, and Ecosystems: Understanding Learning through Metaphor,
pages 27–43.

cesses of the mind. If you can build things that function like the mind, you have a model for the mind. Lachman, Lachman, and Butterfield (1979) explained,

> Computers take symbolic input, recode it, make decisions about it, and give back symbolic output. By analogy, that is most of what cognitive psychology is about. It is about how people take in information, how they recode and remember it, how they make decisions, how they transform their internal knowledge states, and how they translate these states into behavioral output. (p. 99)

To understand the *mind as computer* metaphor, it helps to understand a few things about the computer. In a basic sense, computer-processing hardware consists of a central processing unit (CPU), random access memory (RAM), storage, and various input devices (such as a keyboard and mouse). Let us look at a simple example. In 1987, my parents bought a Macintosh SE. It had a 9" built-in black and white screen. Its CPU was a Motorola MC6800. It had 4 MB RAM, a 400 MB disc drive, and a 40 MB hard drive (bonus option!).

Here is how it worked: If I were forced to write an essay, I would open the MacWrite program and use the mouse and keyboard to enter text into a document. This process of entering information into a computer is called *encoding*. The CPU ran the program and system software and allowed me to create the essay. The functionality of the CPU was reliant on the amount of RAM or temporary memory available. The CPU draws on this memory to perform its functions, but nothing is saved permanently in RAM. I learned this over and over the hard way. I would spend hours writing a single paragraph, then the computer would crash and my writing would be gone forever.

If I wanted to save anything, I had to use the disc drive as we filled up the 40 MB hard drive quickly (a single program today, such as Microsoft Word, is over 50 MB). Thus, I would insert a 3.5" hard plastic disc, save my document on this disc, and then inevitably lose the disc. Saving information permanently on a disc or hard drive is called *storage*. On those rare occasions when I did not lose the disc, I could stick it back in the disc drive and open the document. This process of bringing information from storage back "online" where I could use the CPU to modify it in RAM is called *retrieval*. By the way, losing your work because you did not save it is called *#$!&#!@!*.

By 1988, I was in college rooming with two friends, and we shared a computer and discs. I think we shared discs just so we could get a laugh out of naming files things like "MattIsAButthead" or "CarlosEatsDirt." We had no printer, but we did have a good friend named Jadi who had access to a printer. Jadi was cute, and I secretly had a crush on her. Well, secret to her anyway. My two friends were not in the dark and liked to give files titles like "KevsHeadSpins4Jadilyn." Well, you can guess where this story is going. One day I came back from class and asked where the green disc was.

Carlos: Jadi has it to print a paper for me.

Me: (freaking out): Carlos, did you change the name of your KevsHead-
       Spins4Jadilyn file?

Carlos: What? Oh! Wait, that was on that disc? Yes it was! [falls over laugh-
       ing].

Me: You're a butthead.

Things turned out ok. Jadi and I eventually got married. Go green disc.

MAKING SENSE OF THE METAPHOR

The Information Processing Model

The Information Processing (IP) model, first proposed by Atkinson and Shiffrin (1968), is a theoretical model of the mind's memory systems that explains
how information is processed by and between these systems. Figure 3.1 presents
a version of the IP model illustrating parallels to the computer.

The first step in processing information is receiving information through the
senses (e.g., eyes, ears). The senses are equivalent to input devices on a computer

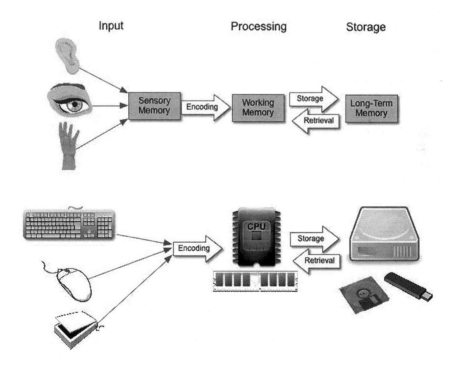

FIGURE 3.1.   Parallels Between the Human and Computer Information Processing
Systems. Note: Image Created Using *Inspiration*®.

(e.g., keyboard, mouse). Information from the senses is filtered through *sensory memory* and into *working memory*.

Sensory memory is unique to humans and does not have a clear parallel in the computer. It captures an imprint of all the information coming in through the senses—all the sights, sounds, tastes, and sensations. This information is mostly held for just a fraction of a second before it is deleted. A very small portion of the information is passed on to working memory. The focus of our attention largely determines what is passed on, and, thus, all the irrelevant information coming in through our senses (e.g., the feel of our clothing, ambient noise) is filtered out and does not clutter up our working memory. It does not always work that smoothly, but more on that later.

Working memory is equivalent to the computer's CPU. You can think of working memory as what is "up and running." Whatever information you are thinking about is in your working memory. Working memory processes information held in *short-term memory*, which corresponds to RAM. That is, short-term memory refers to the capacity to hold information in consciousness. Working memory is the processing and manipulation of information in consciousness.

Today's computers can do many procedures and process huge amounts of information at once. Unfortunately, human working memory is quite limited due to the limited capacity of our short-term memory. To understand such limits, try doing the activities in Box 3.1. How many digits was the longest number string you were able to recall? How many words were you able to recall? Based on numerous experiments like these, early cognitive researchers proposed that our short-term memory could deal with about seven chunks of information at a time, plus or minus two (Miller, 1956). So if you consider each digit or word a chunk, most people can recall between five and nine digits or words[2]. With practice, we can often do much better by creating bigger chunks. For example, memorizing number pairs instead of individual digits or associating words in an image so they become a single chunk. In fact, we nearly always do some chunking, and modern cognitive researchers suggest that our short-term memory capacity is less than the "magic number seven" when prevented from chunking (Cowan, 2001).

Short-term memory is also limited in duration. Like RAM, short-term memory is temporary memory, and anything not stored is lost once you stop thinking about it. Cognitive researchers estimate that our short-term memory holds most information for 10 to 15 seconds unless we keep verbally repeating, or rehearsing, it (Goldstein, 2015). Note that the scientific definition of short-term memory is very different from the colloquial definition. In everyday language, we use short-term memory to refer to memories that we retain for a short period before forgetting—maybe a couple days or weeks. In the scientific community, short-term memory refers exclusively to information being held in consciousness. Recalling infor-

---

[2] Although the complexity of the chunk can be an influence. For instance, we typically recall more number digits than words and more short words than long words.

Box 3.1

Cognitive researchers studied working memory through memory recall tests like these below.

Instructions: Read the number string just once and then see if you can recall the full number sequence without looking. Do one number string at a time.

Instructions: Read each word just once and then see how many of the words you can recall without looking.

6821	Basket	Flower
93412	France	Phone
5463728	Yellow	Neighbor
16289347	Boss	Shoe
316824937	Sandwich	Snow
4794382156		

---

mation, even after a minute of not thinking about it, requires the next step in the memory system: long-term memory.

Long-term memory is like a hard drive or other storage device. Information can be transferred from working memory into long-term memory and later recalled from long-term memory back into working memory—just as a file can be stored on a hard drive and later modified.

Our long-term memory is unlimited in terms of both capacity and duration. Our brains are more impressive than even the most advanced computers in terms of storage capacity. Go humans! However, this does not mean that all the information stored in long-term memory is permanent or accessible. In fact, a great failing of our education system is that we retain so little of the information we store in long-term memory. Chapter 4 focuses on this issue and provides insight on how we can process information so it can be retained and retrieved.

There is quite a bit more complexity to the Information Processing model. Cognitive and neuroscience researchers are continually adding to our understanding of information processing systems in the brain. For example, Baddeley and Hitch (1974) proposed a dual-processing model in which working memory includes a *phonological loop* and a *visuospatial scratchpad*. The former deals with verbal information and the later with visuo-spatial information. Both of these, as well as our processing decisions, are governed by a *central executive*. Modern researchers emphasize the interaction between working and long-term memory. Working memory is a process that emerges from the activation of many parts of the brain, including memory stores. However, a basic understanding of the brain's memory systems is sufficient for comprehending the fundamental learning principles discussed later in this chapter and in chapter 4.

Glitches in the Machine

One of the ways we can understand the normal functioning of the brain is by studying cases of abnormal functioning. In this section, I review three such cases.

As explained above, our sensory memory captures an imprint of all the information coming in through our senses, and then a very small portion of this information is filtered into our working memory. Typically, a small chunk of relevant information is passed on and a huge mass of irrelevant information is filtered out. What if the filter was broken?

Temple Grandin's unique account of her experience growing up with autism may shine light on this question. Temple's story was popularized in the Oliver Sacks book *An Anthropologist on Mars*. Her story is quite remarkable. She offers a level of introspection that is rare for autistic people, and she has also achieved great success as a professor of animal science. But her childhood was not easy, and the struggles seemed to be at least partly associated with a faulty filter[3].

Temple's brain did not seem to automatically filter irrelevant information. Sacks (1995) explains, "Temple describes her world as one of sensations heightened, sometimes to an excruciating degree ... she speaks of her ears, at the age of two or three, as helpless microphones, transmitting everything, irrespective of relevance, at full, overwhelming volume" (p. 254). Temple learned to compensate by focusing intently on a single object or activity. Sacks wrote:

> She soon developed an immense power of concentration, a selectivity of attention so intense that it could create a world of its own, a place of calm and order in the chaos and tumult: "I could sit on the beach for hours dribbling sand through my fingers and fashioning miniature mountains," she writes. "Each particle of sand intrigued me as though I were a scientist looking through a microscope. Other times I scrutinized each line in my finger, following one as if it were a road on a map." (pp. 154–155)

It is as if Temple had to develop a way of conscious filtering through intense concentration because the natural filtering you and I enjoy was not available.

One of the problems with lots of irrelevant information being filtered into working memory is that it clogs up the gears. As explained previously, our working memory is quite limited. Thus, if irrelevant information is taking up working memory, we do not have much processing power left over to do cognitive work. This is an issue not just for individuals like Temple, but anyone who gets distracted by irrelevant stimuli during a learning task. I think it is fair to say that includes everyone, but the challenge can be greater for individuals with Attention Deficit Disorder (ADD). In the implications section, I discuss strategies for dealing with the limits of working memory and reducing the load on working memory.

---

[3] It is impossible to know what exactly was occurring with her memory systems. A "faulty filter" is a probable explanation but not a certain one. Abnormalities farther along in the memory system may also have played a role.

What if the problem is not with the transfer of information *into* working memory but the transfer of information *out* of working memory (i.e., moving it into long-term memory)? Some years ago, I found myself sitting in a camp chair at a park holding a paper cup half full of ice cream and wondering, *where did I get this ice cream? Have I been eating it? Where am I and what am I doing here? How did I get here?* My son walked by in his soccer uniform. *Did he have a soccer game today? When did he start playing soccer?* Turns out, I had been playing flag football and got kicked in the head. I was a bit woozy, and we decided to take a break and eat ice cream. I remembered none of this.

As I tried to make sense of my situation, my memories kept slipping away. It was as if I could not quite form a memory without it fading away into a dream. I would talk briefly with my wife, and seconds later my memory of the conversation became all fuzzy. I did not know if the conversation really happened and could not quite recall it. It just hung there on the edges of my consciousness the way some dreams do when you wake in the morning. Every 10 or 15 seconds, the immediate past faded into a blurry haze[4].

Luckily, I got better within 24 hours, and I got a sense of what it is like to struggle to form memories. Specifically, I experienced what it is like to be impaired in transferring information from working memory to long-term memory. In doing so, I got a glimpse of life as Henry Molaison.

Henry Molaison, or HM[5] as he is known in the research literature, is one of the most famous cases in neuropsychology. Henry suffered from severe epileptic seizures, and in 1953, a doctor removed sections of his brain believed to be causing the seizures. The surgery was successful in reducing seizures, but the cure came with a tragic side effect: Henry lost the ability to create new memories.

In her book on Henry, *Permanent Present Tense*, Suzanne Corkin (2013) writes of a conversation she had with had with Henry:

"What do you do during a typical day?"
"See, that's tough—what I don't…I don't remember things."
"Do you know what you did yesterday?"
"No, I don't."
"How about this morning?"
"I don't even remember that."
"Could you tell me what you had for lunch today?"
"I don't know, tell you the truth, I'm not—"
"What do you think you'll do tomorrow?"
"Whatever's beneficial," he said in his friendly, direct way.

---

[4] There are a few things that still puzzle me about this experience. How am I able to remember the sensation of my brain not forming memories? How do I remember sitting in that chair with ice cream—shouldn't this memory have faded like the others? I don't have good answers but I think perhaps the shock of finding myself in that chair formed a stronger memory (see chapter 4) and likely that memory initially was fuzzy but I have reconstructed it over time (see chapter 5).

[5] His full name was not revealed unto after his death in 2008.

"Good answer," I said. "Have we ever met before, you and I?"

"Yes, I think we have."

"Where?"

"Well, in high school?"

"In high school?"

"Yes."

"What high school?"

"In East Hartford."

"Have we ever met any place besides high school?"

Henry paused. "Tell you the truth, I can't—no. I don't think so." (p. xiii)

Corkin first met Henry as a graduate student at McGill University. At the time of this interview, she had been working with Henry for thirty years.

Henry's surgery removed most of the hippocampus on both sides of his brain. We now know, largely as a consequence of Henry's surgery, that the hippocampus is critical to memory processes. Corkin and others conducted many studies with Henry to understand his memory functioning. They determined his short-term memory was fine. Short-term in this case refers specifically to the "RAM" component of working memory (i.e., his capacity to hold information in consciousness). For example, he could perform a digit span test like that in Box 3.1 at a normal level. Henry failed, however, at complex working memory tasks that required drawing on long-term memory. And, as the conversation with Corkin illustrates, Henry failed to retain information over time. His limit was about 60 seconds. After that, any memories formed or information learned was gone. As Corkin stated, Henry was "trapped in a permanent present tense" (2013, p. 33).

Henry did retain memories from before his surgery. His long-term memory was not disabled by the surgery, and he was able to recall his prior life and access knowledge he had learned. However, there were significant disruptions. Henry lost memories of events occurring in the years leading up to the surgery (e.g., he did not remember the death of an uncle, which occurred three years prior to the surgery). In addition, Henry struggled to recall details of the events he did remember. For example, he remembered his parents and the life events they shared but, when pressed, was unable to provide details of these life events. Two exceptions were discovered. Henry was able to give a rich account of his first experience flying in a plane and his first experience smoking a cigarette at age ten.

Interestingly, Henry did not have trouble recalling knowledge and facts learned prior to his surgery—just trouble with recalling details of personal experience. This discrepancy between Henry's memory of life episodes and learned information helped confirm that the brain has different long-term memory systems: *episodic memory*, which deals with life events, and *semantic memory*, which deals with information.

Two other memory systems were also confirmed and further understood by Henry's case: *declarative* and *procedural* memory. Even though Henry was not able to store new memories, he did learn new things. For example, he improved measurably at a mirror-tracing task over the course of three days. This task, which is difficult for anyone, required Henry to trace a star with a pencil when he could only see the star and his hand in a mirror. Henry got much better at tracing the star even though he never remembered previously performing the task. He also improved as a memory test subject (e.g., he understood the test scheme better, and was more on task) even though he never improved on the memory tests themselves and did not remember taking them.

From these results, Corkin and colleagues concluded that the declarative memory system is distinct from the procedural memory system, and the former was compromised while the later remained in tact. Declarative or explicit memory is memory of what can be consciously recalled. Post-surgery, Henry was unable to consciously recall any memories created after the surgery. Procedural memory is unconscious memory associated with the performance of tasks, such as riding a bike. This memory system remained functional and was virtually the only working link going from working memory to long-term memory.

Henry's memory deficit seriously disrupted his life and his ability to be a self-sufficient adult. However, Henry remained positive and lived a largely stress-free life, thanks to his inability to remember anything beyond 60 seconds. His contribution to neuropsychology was incalculable and is ongoing, as he donated his brain to science. Nevertheless, the consequences of his surgery were quite tragic, and I would not recommend removal of the hippocampus as a stress-reduction strategy.

The cases of Temple Grandin and Henry Molaison illustrate problems related primarily to the transfer of information between memory systems. But what if there is damage to working memory itself? Severe damage would result in a coma, but minor damage can have some interesting effects. Take the case of LE as reported by Wilson, Baddeley, and Young (1999): LE was a gifted sculptor who created lifelike sculptures of human figures. After contracting a disease affecting the central nervous system (systemic lupus erythematosus), LE began to experience cognitive difficulties. One problem was getting dressed. LE found this difficult, not because she experienced any physical difficulties, but "because she could not 'see' what things went together" (p. 122). That is, she could not imagine in her mind how different articles of clothing would look when worn together. She could not conjure the image in her mind.

She also had difficulties navigating in a car. At times, she would get lost and call her husband or daughter to rescue her. During an appointment at the Cognition and Brain Sciences Unit in Cambridge, LE was asked how to get from her current location to the motorway. Despite the fact that the route was simple and she had just driven it, LE could not visualize and describe the route. She explained, "I can't do it. I can get there stage by stage but I can't tell you how" (p. 122).

Perhaps the most interesting symptoms related to her art. If asked to copy a drawing placed before her, she could do so perfectly. But if asked to draw even simple images without a copy to look at, she struggled tremendously. Commenting on this, LE explained, "I can't see where things come. For example, I cannot think where the eyes go or where the foot goes and I have to keep checking where the thumbs are. I cannot keep work in my head the way I used to" (p. 122). *Can't think where the eyes go?* Her sculptures changed from lifelike to abstract representations with some forms approximating a human shape. LE further explained, "My 'mind's eye' is faulty. I've got the knowledge but it doesn't come to me. I can't hold the image" (p. 122).

Based on these symptoms and results from various tests, Wilson and colleagues concluded that LE suffered disruptions in the component of working memory responsible for generating and holding an image. Researchers refer to this component as the visuospatial scratchpad. Thus, thanks to a functioning visuospatial scratchpad, you are able to imagine and visualize things. This may seem minor, but think about it for moment. Never being able to recall a beautiful sunset you just watched. Never being able to recall the image of your daughter's first soccer goal. Anything not captured on film would be lost. I would carry a camera everywhere.

IMPLICATIONS

Chapter 4 delves into the nature of long-term memory and addresses implications associated with that part of the memory system. In this chapter, I focus on implications stemming from the nature (and limitations) of our working memory. These implication include strategies for reducing cognitive load and, possibly, increasing our working memory. I also raise the question of whether we are more than a mere computer program.

Reduce the Load on Working Memory

Cognitive Load Theory (Chandler & Sweller, 1991; Sweller, 1988) considers the educational implications of our limited working memory. "Cognitive load" refers to the amount of information that can be held in working memory, and central to the theory is the identification of three different types of cognitive load associated with learning: intrinsic, extraneous, and germane (Sweller, Van Merrienboer, & Paas, 1998).

Intrinsic cognitive load refers to the degree of inherent complexity in the to-be-learned information. It is the load intrinsic to the content itself. Complexity is defined as the number of elements that have to be learned simultaneously. For example, basic multiplication has low intrinsic cognitive load because you only have to hold a couple elements in your mind at once. Economic theory, on the other hand, has high cognitive load because you have to hold many variables in your mind at once and consider their interaction.

Even though intrinsic cognitive load is a characteristic of the content, novices will experience much more intrinsic cognitive load than experts. This is because experts develop domain-specific schemas allowing them to bring together a number of disparate elements. Where novices perceive separate elements, experts perceive patterns (see Chapter 4). Many times, when students struggle to understand a complex idea or procedure, they conclude they are not smart enough. This is a false and self-defeating conclusion. The struggle is not because they aren't smart, but because the intrinsic cognitive load of the content is a mismatch with their current level of expertise. They simply need to spend time developing schemas in the domain, and then their working memory will not be over-taxed by the content.

Intrinsic cognitive load cannot be manipulated, but it can be carefully sequenced and matched to learners. Teachers can break down complex content with high intrinsic cognitive load into simpler sub-ideas. Novices first learn these sub-ideas independently and later combine them. Teachers need to be thoughtful about matching the complexity of the content to the prior knowledge backgrounds of their students. Learners themselves can also sequence content. For example, when struggling to understand a complex idea in a college course, students can identify the different parts of the complex idea, study these parts separately, then go back to making sense of the complex idea. By studying the parts separately, they will build schemas that will reduce the cognitive load experienced when dealing with the complex idea. Another effective strategy is to automatize basic skills (i.e., learn and repeat basic skills until their performance become automatic). Automatized skills can be executed almost effortlessly, thus freeing up working memory for more complex tasks.

In addition to the intrinsic cognitive load, a learning situation also involves cognitive demands associated with the instructional or learning tasks (e.g., listening to a lecture; completing a science lab). These cognitive demands reflect extrinsic cognitive load and are of two varieties: extraneous and germane cognitive load.

Extraneous cognitive load is the amount of working memory resources allocated to task demands that *do not* aid learning. Think of extraneous cognitive load as task complexities that just get in the way of learning. An example would be instructions so confusing and onerous that it takes more work to figure out the instructions than to learn the content. Another example would be textbooks in which the basic content is obscured by long, awkward sentences with pompous vocabulary (hmm, that never happens).

Germane cognitive load is the amount of working memory resources allocated to task demands that *do* aid learning. Not all task demands get in the way of learning. Some of them aid learning; in fact, they are the very means of learning. For example, memorizing math facts takes up cognitive load, but this load directly contributes to learning math.

An analogy helps clarify the difference between extraneous and germane cognitive load. Suppose the goal is to get in better shape, and the designated task is to exercise at the gym. The germane load would be difficulties that are part of the actual workout, such as lifting weights or running on a treadmill. The extraneous load would include complexities and difficulties interfering with the workout, such as membership requirements, restricted hours, or faulty equipment.

We can facilitate learning for others and ourselves by reducing extraneous cognitive load and maintaining an appropriate level of germane cognitive load. Strategies for reducing extraneous cognitive load include:

- Avoiding distractions and irrelevant information.
- Integrating information.
- Taking advantage of working memory's dual processing capability.
- Using direct instruction instead of pure discovery learning for novices.

Distractions and irrelevant information take up precious working memory space without contributing to learning. For example, "seductive details" are interesting facts or anecdotes unrelated to the content of a passage of text or a lecture. Research finds that seductive details undermine learning (Harp & Mayer, 1998) even though we typically learn much better when interested (Hidi, 1990). In a similar vein, unnecessary details in a textbook or lecture can interfere with comprehending the big ideas. When we are barraged with information, we often do not have enough working memory space leftover to process content with high intrinsic cognitive load. Distractions in the learning environment also take up cognitive load. Such distractions can include disorganized space and procedures, technology not associated with learning, and the behavior of students.

It is important that teachers do what they can to reduce distractions and irrelevant information, but students also play an important role. When attending class, reading a textbook, or studying materials, it is easy to get distracted by irrelevant things in the environment or your own mind (i.e., daydreaming). These distractions reduce available working memory and inhibit learning. When possible, arrange your learning environment to avoid distractions. I have yet to convince my own kids of the value of doing so. One of my daughters always studied while watching Netflix. I tried to explain the consequences of dedicating half your working memory to a TV show while trying to do homework. Her retort was that most of the homework was such low-level busy work it only required half a brain anyway.

Another very important skill to develop as a learner is the ability to sift through the mass of information being presented in a lecture or textbook and focus on the most important ideas. Often we do not have enough working memory space available to take in everything. Thus, it becomes very important that we allocate our working memory to processing the most important content. You can do this by asking yourself questions such as "What is the big picture? What is the central idea? What is the idea that ties the details together?"

Teachers and instructional designers can also reduce extraneous cognitive load by integrating information. For example, a figure or diagram can convey a lot of information in a holistic way requiring relatively little working memory. But we do not always optimize diagrams for easy processing. Instead of creating simple, self-explanatory diagrams, we often surround them with additional labels and explanations. Switching back and forth between reading text and studying a diagram takes up twice as much cognitive load. Researchers refer to this as the *split-attention effect*—your attention and working memory resources are split between two sources of information.

A more effective method would be to take advantage of working memory's *dual processing capability*. In addition to the visuospatial scratchpad, working memory includes a phonological loop, which is responsible for processing verbal information. These two components of working memory have largely independent capacities. This means we can process more information simultaneously if some of the information is aural and some is visual. Thus, an animation with audio explanation is more brain-friendly than an animation with a visual text explanation. The video with text results in the split-attention effect because the visuospatial scratchpad is forced to process both sources of information. The video with audio draws on both components of working memory, so more information can be processed without increasing cognitive load.

Teachers can also reduce extraneous cognitive load by using direct instruction instead of pure discovery learning for novices (although this strategy is controversial, as you will see shortly). Direct instruction refers to such strategies as lecturing on content, explaining how to solve a problem, and modeling correct performance[6]. Pure discovery learning involves giving students a problem to solve or topic to study and providing minimal support and guidance. The emphasis is on having students discover solutions and concepts on their own. For example, prior to giving instruction on particular content, a science teacher may have students explore the content in a group through some sort of lab work. Thus, students are simultaneously engaging in problem solving and learning new content. Working memory dedicated to solving problems is not available for learning the new content.

If the content has high intrinsic cognitive load and the learners are novices in the area of study, then students may struggle to learn the content. Backing up this claim, some research finds that students learn new content more efficiently when provided with direct instruction instead of unguided discovery learning (Kirschner, Sweller, & Clark, 2006). For example, novices presented with worked examples (examples of problems being worked out) often perform better than students who were asked to discover the solution on their own (Kirschner et al., 2006).

However, arguing that direction instruction is always superior to discovery learning is controversial for a few reasons. First, even though problem solving takes up working memory, it can contribute to content learning. For example, Schwartz and Martin (2004) found that students provided with an opportunity

---

[6] The Direct Instruction program mentioned in Chapter 2 is just one example of what direct instruction can be.

for unguided discovery were better prepared to learn from a worked example and apply their learning to a novel problem than students who received explicit instruction on the content prior to the worked example. Chapters 4 and 6 also explain how learning through problem solving and exploration can contribute to long-term retention and conceptual change. Second, rarely do teachers use pure, unguided discovery learning. Instead, current instructional models associated with discovery learning (e.g., problem-based learning, inquiry learning, constructivist models) place heavy emphasis on teacher guidance and scaffolding, which reduces the cognitive load (Hmelo-Silver, Duncan, & Chinn, 2007; Schmidt, Loyens, van Gog, & Paas, 2007). Third, content learning is far from the only goal of discovery learning models. Other goals include developing problem-solving and collaboration skills, and encouraging self-directed learning habits and intrinsic motivation (Hmelo-Silver, 2004; Kuhn, 2007).

Reducing extraneous cognitive load does not mean that we should always simplify learning tasks. Sometimes we want learning tasks to be more complex and difficult because the difficulty promotes additional learning (i.e., the difficulty is associated with germane but not extraneous cognitive load). For example, Salomon (1993) designed a computer-based writing tool that increased germane cognitive load by complicating the story-writing process through such strategies as requiring students to interact with a series of planning tools and prompts. The writing tool transformed the simple process of free-association story telling into a more complex process of planning, self-diagnosis, and composition revision. At the same time, the writing tool reduced extraneous cognitive load by providing memory aids. High school students who used the writing tool exerted greater effort in writing and, as evidence that this effort was associated with germane load, they produced better stories—both when using the writing tool and, later, when writing without its aid.

Increase the Capacity?

Short-term memory is fixed. But working memory? We might be able to increase that with training. As a reminder, short-term memory is the capacity to hold information in consciousness. Working memory is the ability to process or manipulate information in consciousness. For a long time, researchers believed that working memory had a fixed capacity due to its reliance on short-term memory. But more recent research calls this conclusion into question—which is huge because working memory is at the heart of fluid intelligence. Fluid intelligence is the capacity to solve problems and think logically, independent of acquired knowledge

In his book *Smarter: The New Science of Building Brain Power*, Dan Hurley (2013) reviews recent research and chronicles his own exuberant experience as a brain-building guinea pig. As Hurley explains, scholars had long established that no amount of training improves short-term memory. Individuals can clearly get better at short-term memory tasks, but the improvement does not transfer to other short-term memory tasks. For example, in a well-known study, Ericsson, Chase, and Faloon (1980) found that an undergraduate, S.F., was able to dramatically increase his ability to recite back a string of numbers through training. Indeed, he was able to perform at the level of a memory expert and recite back nearly 80 digits (remember 7 is average). However, when tasked with reciting back letters instead of numbers, his recall dropped right back down to 6. S.F. did not increase his short-term memory. Rather, he developed mnemonic strategies for remembering number strings.

Scholars assumed working memory was equally fixed until recently, when a few started testing the ability to improve working memory through training. Working memory tests differ from short-term memory tests in that they require the manipulation of information (e.g., multiplying numbers instead of holding number strings in memory). One such test is the N-back, in which participants listen to a continuous string of letters. They are expected to press a button every time they hear the same letter repeated. At the 1-back level, participants press the button every time they hear a letter twice in a row. At the 2-back level, they press the button every time they hear the repeat of a letter spoken two steps back (i.e., with one other letter in between the repeated letters), and so on. By design, the task gets very hard very quickly, so it taps the limits of working memory.

Jaeggi, Buschkuehl, Jonides, and Perrig (2008) trained university students on a dual N-back test and measured their fluid intelligence before and after training. Not only did the students improve their fluid intelligence scores, but also their improvement increased with the amount of training received. Students receiving the maximum amount of training, 19 days, increased their fluid intelligence scores *more than 40 percent!* As Hurley (2013) notes in his book, these results were stunning to a scientific community that believed working memory was fixed, and the study made headlines around the world.

Although the research is still in its infancy, scholars have now linked other activities to the development of working memory and fluid intelligence, including exercise, learning to play a musical instrument, and meditation. The effect may be greater for those with lower initial fluid intelligence.

Hurley himself decided to go all in as a test subject. He started training on the N-back and Lumosity (a commercial company offering mind games that tax working memory similarly to the N-back), exercising regularly, taking lute lessons, and wearing a nicotine patch (nicotine was also linked to fluid intelligence in some studies). After three and half months, his fluid intelligence score increased by 16.4 percent. What do we make of all this? It seems we do have some influence over the capabilities of our working memory. We can get smarter with effort.

Are We More Than a Program?

As I mentioned previously, we have a fascination with the relationship between computers and humans. What are the implications of Robert Epstein falling for a chatterbot? Are we anything more than programs running on organic software?

"Ah, but we are self-aware and computers are not," you object. Maybe. Maybe not. Prominent philosopher Daniel Dennett (1991) agues there is nothing special about consciousness, nothing magical about the mind. It does not arise from a soul or any other metaphysical form. It is simply brain activity; billions of neurons doing their electro-chemical thing. That's it. No single cell has consciousness, but together they create the *illusion* of consciousness. In this view, we really are no different than the functioning of a bunch of computers all linked together.

What will happen if we link ourselves to computers? In a 2014 TED talk, Ray Kurzweil stated,

> Twenty years from now, we'll have nanobots…go into our brain through the capillaries and basically connect our neocortex to a synthetic neocortex in the cloud providing an extension of our neocortex…[O]ur thinking, then, will be a hybrid of biological and non-biological thinking, but the non-biological portion is subject to my law of accelerating returns. It will grow exponentially.

This is way beyond *The Matrix*. This is having your brain supplemented by nearly infinite computing power! Will we still be human?

I do not have the answers to these questions, but the older I get, the more I am in need of an upgrade.

REFERENCES

Atkinson, R. C., & Shiffrin, R. M. (1968). Human memory: A proposed system and its control processes. In K. W. Spencer & J. T. Spence (Eds.), *Advances in the psychology of learning and motivation research and theory, Vol. 2* (pp. 89–195). New York, NY: Academic Press.

Baddeley, A. D., & Hitch, G. (1974). Working memory. In G. H. Bower (Ed.), *The psychology of learning and motivation, Vol. 8* (pp. 47–89). New York, NY: Academic Press.

Chandler, P., & Sweller, J. (1991). Cognitive load theory and the format of instruction. *Cognition and Instruction, 8*, 293–332. doi:10.1207/s1532690xci0804_2

Corkin, S. (2013). *Permanent present tense: The unforgettable life of the amnesic patient, H.M.* New York, NY: Basic Books.

Cowan, N. (2001). The magical number 4 in short-term memory: A reconsideration of mental storage capacity. *Behavioral and Brain Sciences, 24*, 87–185. doi:10.1017/S0140525X01003922

Dennett, D. C. (1991). *Consciousness explained.* Boston, MA: Little, Brown & Co.

Epstein, R. (2007). From Russia, with love: How I got fooled (and somewhat humiliated) by a computer. *Scientific American Mind, 18*(5), 16–17. doi:10.1038/scientificamericanmind1007-16

Ericcson, K. A., Chase, W. G., & Faloon, S. (1980). Acquisition of a memory skill. *Science, 208*, 1181–1182. doi:10.1126/science.7375930

Goldstein, E. B. (2015). *Cognitive psychology: Connecting mind, research and everyday experience, Fourth Ed.* Stamford, CT: Cengage Learning.

Harp, S. F., & Mayer, R. E. (1998). How seductive details do their damage: A theory of cognitive interest in science learning. *Journal of Educational Psychology, 90*, 414–434. doi:10.1037/0022-0663.90.3.414

Hidi, S. (1990). Interest and its contribution as a mental resource for learning. *Review of Educational Research, 60*, 549–571. doi:10.3102/00346543060004549

Hmelo-Silver, C. (2004). Problem-based learning: What and how do students learn? *Educational Psychology Review, 16*, 235–266. doi:10.1023/B:EDPR.0000034022.16470. f3

Hmelo-Silver, C. E., Duncan, R. G., & Chinn, C. A. (2007). Scaffolding and achievement in problem-based and inquiry learning: A response to Kirschner, Sweller, and Clark (2006). *Educational Psychologist, 42*, 99–107. doi:10.1080/00461520701263368

Hurley, D. (2013). *Smarter: The new science of building brain power.* New York, NY: Plume.

Jaeggi, S. M., Buschkuehl, M., Jonides, J., & Perrig, W. J. (2008). Improving fluid intelligence with training on working memory. *Proceedings of the National Academy of Sciences, 105*(19), 6829–6833. doi:10.1073/pnas.0801268105

Kirschner, P. A., Sweller, J., & Clark, R. E. (2006). Why minimal guidance during instruction does not work: An analysis of the failure of constructivist, discovery, problem-based, experiential, and inquiry-based teaching. *Educational Psychologist, 41*, 75–86. doi:10.1207/s15326985ep4102_1

Kuhn, D. (2007). Is direct instruction an answer to the right question? *Educational Psychologist, 42*, 109–113. doi:10.1080/00461520701263376

Kurzweil, R. (2014). Get ready for hybrid thinking. *TED Talk.* Retrieved from http://www. ted.com/talks/ray_kurzweil_get_ready_for_hybrid_thinking?language=en

Lachman, R., Lachman, J. L., & Butterfield, E. C. (1979). *Cognitive psychology and information processing: An introduction.* Hillsdale, NJ: Lawrence Erlbaum.

Miller, G. A. (1956). The magical number seven, plus or minus two: Some limits on our capacity for processing information. *Psychological Review, 63*(2), 81–97. doi:doi:10.1037/h0043158

Sacks, O. (1995). *An anthropologist on Mars: Seven paradoxical tales.* New York, NY: Vintage Books.

Salomon, G. (1993). On the nature of pedagogic computer tools: The case of the Writing Partner. In S. P. Lajoie & S. J. Derry (Eds.), *Computers as cognitive tools* (pp. 179–196). Hillsdale, NJ: Erlbaum.

Schmidt, H. G., Loyens, M. M., van Gog, T., & Paas, F. (2007). Problem-based learning is compatible with human cognitive architecture: Commentary on Kirschner, Sweller, and Clark (2006). *Educational Psychologist, 42*, 91–97. doi:10.1080/00461520701263350

Schwartz, D. L., & Martin, T. (2004). Inventing to prepare for future learning: The hidden efficiency of encouraging original student production in statistics instruction. *Cognition and Instruction, 22*, 129–184. doi:10.1207/s1532690xci2202_1

Sweller, J. (1988). Cognitive load during problem solving: Effects on learning. *Cognitive Science, 12*, 257–285. doi:10.1016/0364-0213(88)90023-7

Sweller, J., van Merrienboer, J. J. G., & Paas, F. G. W. C. (1998). Cognitive architecture and instructional design. *Educational Psychology Review, 10*, 251–296. doi:10.1023/A:1022193728205

Wilson, B. A., Baddeley, A. D., & Young, A. W. (1999). LE, a person who lost her 'mind's eye.' *Neurocase, 5*, 119–127. doi:10.1080/13554799908415476

CHAPTER 4

MIND AS NETWORK

Our memory can be bizarre. Sometimes we study information for hours only to have it desert us when we most need it—like during that final exam worth half the course grade. Other times we cannot forget memories despite desperate attempts to do so. It is impossible to fully explain the behavior of our individual memories. However, cognitive scientists can tell us a lot about when we are likely to retain or forget information, how we can more effectively retain it, and how teachers can foster long-term retention. In terms of the information processing model, retention involves the ability to store information in long-term memory and later bring it back into working memory. Thus to understand retention, we need to know something about the nature of long-term memory, and the key to understanding the nature of long-term memory is to see it as a network.

There are many networks that could serve as metaphors for the mind: the intertwined roots of mangrove trees, the network of friends and associates that defines a person's "social capital," and so on. I will focus on two networks I find particularly useful for understanding memory: (1) the Internet and (2) a picture as a patterned network.

Think about how information is organized on the Internet compared to a book. Most books organize information in a linear fashion, to be read in one direction from start to finish. The Internet organizes information as a connected network with no predetermined path for reading the information. Instead, information is

Computers, Cockroaches, and Ecosystems: Understanding Learning through Metaphor,
pages 45–66.

Box 4.1

connected via hyperlinks, and individuals navigate sites idiosyncratically by following these links. The more some information is linked to other information, the more likely it is to be read. Highly linked information is also more likely to be found again, because it can be reached by multiple paths. This would be particularly true if Google suddenly ceased to exist (don't panic, it's just a thought experiment). Thus, the more links there are to a webpage, the less likely it is to be lost in cyberspace. Keep that in mind.

A picture is another type of network, a pattern of information. On the following page is a box with five different versions of the same photograph (don't look yet). The top version has been highly pixelated using the pointillize filter in Photoshop™. The next version is slightly less pixelated, and so on until you reach the unaltered photo at the bottom. Turn to the next page and cover the box with a piece of paper. Slide the paper down until the top image is revealed. Try to guess what was photographed. Then slide the paper to reveal the next image and repeat. Keep doing this until you get to the final image.

Unless you have superhero pattern detection powers, the first image was likely just a bunch of squashed dots. The second image probably was not much better. However, at some point, something remarkable happened. The set of images went from being a bunch of dots to an actual picture[1]. You had an "aha" moment in which you thought, "Aha! That's what it is!"

Now, without looking at the images, try to recreate the top image in your mind. Then try to recreate the bottom image. The first image is likely to be a vague image of differently shaded dots. If you could hold the image in your mind, click "print" on the side of your head, and print out that image, it is extremely unlikely that the image would be close to the original (again, unless you are a superhero). However, you likely can recall the image of the bottom picture fairly accurately. If you clicked "print" on your head, the resulting image would be recognizable as a reproduction. Why? Because even though there is far more detail and total information in the bottom image, all the information fits together in one holistic pattern. Information that is part of a pattern is far easier to process and recall. Keep that in mind.

MAKING SENSE OF THE METAPHOR

The Importance of Connections

The network is not just a metaphor for the mind but a literal description. The brain is a physical network of neural connections. Within this network, information is stored as a series of associations. Consequently, connections are key to the storage, retention, and recall of information.

Whether new information is stored at all in long-term memory is largely a consequence of the degree to which it connects to the existing network. In some ways, the existing network is like a net that catches familiar or relatable information while unfamiliar information passes right through. But even information caught by the net may not be retrievable because it gets lost in the vastness of our existing knowledge network. The number and quality of connections matter a lot in terms of being able to recall information from long-term memory. Here the *mind as Internet* metaphor comes in handy. Just as a highly linked webpage is less likely to be lost in cyberspace, so highly connected information is less likely to be lost in your neural space. If those links are to prominent websites, so much the better.

---

[1] By the way, these are some bighorn sheep I happened upon while fishing one day.

The way Google searches work helps clarify this point. When you search for a term, say "long-term memory," how does Google rank the thousands of results? The process is complex, but a key determinant is the PageRank. Each page has a PageRank calculated by the number and quality of links to the page. Thus, if we have a page with a lot of other pages pointing (i.e., linking) to it, our page will have a higher PageRank. In addition, the PageRank of the pointing pages influences the PageRank of our page. For example, CNN.com has a high PageRank because many other pages on the Internet link to that site. If CNN.com linked to our page, then the PageRank of our page would greatly increase. The higher our PageRank, the more likely our page is to show up at the top of a listing of Google search results. This search strategy is based on the assumption that links equal importance.

In a similar way, information in your brain gets a degree of "recallability" based on the number and quality of other information linking to it. Information with lots of links is more likely to come up in a memory search. Links to other highly linked information are even better. Put another way, the more central some information is to a network of knowledge, the better we can recall it.

For an illustration of the relationship between memory and connections, consider the cases of Kim Peek and Mr. S. Both possessed extraordinary memories, and both intuitively processed information in a highly connected manner. Kim Peek was an autistic savant who taught himself to read at 16 months, memorized the entire Bible by age seven, and could accurately recall the contents of more than 12,000 books by the end of his life in 2009. He could read a typical book in about an hour, scanning the left page with his left eye and the right page with his right eye, and recall almost everything he read. Screenwriter Barry Morrow met Peek at an Association of Retarded Citizens meeting. Morrow was so enthralled he wrote a movie about a character modeled after Peek. The character, named Raymond Babbitt, was played by Dustin Hoffman in the hit movie *Rain Man*.

One fascinating characteristic of Peek's memory was that the cuing of any information set off a chain of associations with other information. In the documentary *The Real Rain Man*, Kim Peek intones the famous first four notes of Beethoven's Fifth symphony, "Da Da Da Daaaaa." Then he remarks, "Beethoven. Fifth. Morse code. Dot dot dot dash. V for victory. Winston Churchill." This might sound like rambling, but it is only because we do not intuitively see the connections between information as Peek did. He saw "Da Da Da Daaaaa" as Morse code (dot, dot, dot, dash) for the letter "V" which also happens to be the Roman numeral for five, connecting back to Beethoven's Fifth symphony. "V" is also prominent in the "V for Victory" campaign promoted by Winston Churchill. For Peek, all these connections were immediate and intuitive. We cannot begin to explain the workings of Peek's brain. However, it seems probable that this intuitive connectedness of information played a role in his remarkable memory.

In his book, *The Mind of a Mnemonist: A Little Book about a Vast Memory*, A. R. Luria (1968) provides an astonishing account of Mr. S—a man with a seemingly limitless memory. In 1937, Luria, a renowned Russian psychologist, read several stanzas from Dante's *The Divine Comedy* to Mr. S. with slight pauses between words. Mr. S. was able to reproduce the stanzas perfectly despite the fact that he had no knowledge of Italian and the stanzas were read in Dante's native Italian. Now, here's the real kicker: Mr. S. was able to again reproduce these stanzas perfectly *15 years later!* Luria gave Mr. S. many such memory tests and always got the same result. Mr. S. could view or hear long lists of words, nonsense syllables, or numbers once and recall them perfectly, not just minutes or days later, but *decades* later. Luria concluded there were no discernable limits to Mr. S.'s memory.

As with Kim Peek, we cannot fully explain how Mr. S.'s brain worked, but connections were central to what Luria discovered. First, Mr. S. had what psychologists call "synesthesia," meaning, his senses were connected. Sounds had images and colors associated with them; images had distinctive tastes, and so on. Often an object would elicit a reaction from all his senses. For example, he stated, "How could I possibly forget [the way back]? After all, there is this fence. It has such a salty taste and feels so rough; furthermore, it has such a sharp, piercing sound" (Luria, 1968, p. 38). Once Mr. S. met Lev Vygotsky (whose theory of learning is discussed in chapter 7) and remarked, "What a crumbly, yellow voice you have" (p. 24). Even the sounds of letters created distinctive images of "lines," "blurs," and "splashes," which helped him remember nonsense syllables and words that had no meaning to him (e.g., Hebrew words).

In addition to this synesthesia, words and numbers had concrete, and often elaborate, images associated with them. Each number, for instance, was connected with an image of an individual: "1. This is a proud, well-built man; 2 is a high-spirited woman...7 a man with a mustache; 8 a very stout woman...As for the number 87, what I see is a fat woman and a man twirling his mustache" (p. 31). Likewise, all familiar words were associated with particular, vivid images that popped into his mind when he heard or read them. Mr. S. described what went on in his mind when he was read a sentence about a merchant who sold some amount of fabric:

> As soon as I heard the words *merchant* and *sold*, I saw both the shop and the storekeeper, who was standing behind the counter with only the upper part of his body visible to me. He was dealing with a factory representative. Standing at the door of the shop I could see the buyer, whose back was toward me. When he moved off a little to the left, I saw not only the factory but also some account of books. (p. 64)

For meaningless words, Mr. S. often made connections to words that did have meaning, and used images associated with those words to recall the meaningless words. This is how he memorized stanzas of *The Divine Comedy*. When asked to describe how he recalled the stanzas [the first line reads: Nel mezzo del cammin...], Mr. S. explained,

(Nel)—I was paying my membership dues when there, in the corridor, I caught sight of the ballerina Nel'skaya.

(mezzo)—I myself am a violinist; what I do is set up an image of a man, together with ["together with" in Russian: vmeste] Nel'skaya, who is playing the violin.

(del)—There's a pack of Deli Cigarettes near them.

(cammin)—I set up an image of a fireplace [Russian: kamin] close by. (p. 45–46)

Mr. S. would then walk through his image and read off the lines to the stanza.

Creating and walking through an image such as this was a primary strategy used by Mr. S. When given a series to memorize, he frequently chose a familiar street and distributed the images associated with the words or numbers along the street. When asked to recall the series, he simply took a mental walk down the street and read off the images he had placed in doorways, windows, fences, and so on. If asked to recall a series in reverse order, he started the walk from the other end. In administering memory tasks, Luria discovered that the only mistakes Mr. S. made were ones of perception instead of memory. That is, when Mr. S. missed an item in recalling a series, it was not because he forgot the item, but because he did not see it on his mental walk. For example, Mr. S. explained how he omitted the word "egg" in recalling a series: "I put it up against a white wall and it blended in with the background. How could I possibly spot a white egg up against a white wall?" (p. 36).

Reminiscent of Kim Peek, the images brought to mind by words and numbers often elicited a cascade of associated images, as in this example:

I'm reading the Bible. There's a passage in which Saul appears at the house of a certain sorceress. When I started reading this, the witch described in "The Night Before Christmas" appeared to me. And when I read further, I saw the little house in which the story takes place—that is, the image I had of when I was seven years old: the bagel shop and the storage room in the cellar right next to it…Yet it was the Bible I started to read. (p. 115)

To summarize, connections were vital to Mr. S.'s memory processing. Words and numbers were connected to multiple senses through his synesthesia. They were also connected to vibrant images, and these images were embedded in rich, vivid scenes, distributed along familiar locations, and intuitively associated with other images.

The Importance of Patterns.

As the prior section makes clear, retention and recall of information is support-ed by a connected network. Adding pattern and structure to this network further enhances the effectiveness of our memory functioning. Just as dots that coalesce into a picture are easier to recall, so information that fits a pattern is easier to recall. In both cases, individual bits of information are integrated into a whole, which is far easier to process, retain, and recall.

Experts are much more effective than novices at learning new information in their area of expertise. One reason is that they have pre-existing patterns for organizing and retaining the information. A classic study of novice and expert chess players illustrates this point.

Chase and Simon (1973) designed a memory task in which participants were allowed to view a chessboard with pieces at various locations. Under one condition, the chess pieces were arranged randomly on the board. Under a second condition, the board mirrored the middle of an actual game. After five seconds, the board was hidden and participants were asked to recreate the configuration of pieces on a different board. Three players participated in the study: a novice, a Class A player (good but not a master), and a chess master. Each player did the memory task multiple times under each condition. Take a moment to predict how each player did under each condition.

Under the actual game condition, the chess master correctly placed an average of 16 pieces (out of about 25). The Class A player correctly placed an average of 8 and the novice only an average of 4. The fact that those with more expertise did better is probably not that surprising. But here is the interesting part. Under the random placement condition, there was no difference in performance between the three players. Expertise only benefitted memory when the arrangement of pieces came from a real game. Why?

When the arrangement came from an actual game, the chess master saw patterns. These patterns included various attacking and defending configurations and placements that "made sense." The Class A player saw fewer and more limited patterns, and the novice perceived hardly any patterns. Referring back to our metaphor, the chess master was seeing a holistic picture—or at least parts of a picture—whereas the novice was seeing the dots. Seeing the picture makes all the difference.

A similar example comes from American football. Early in a new season, TV pundits like to say "the game is slowing down for him," mainly in reference to a young quarterback who has gained some experience. For example, Aaron Rodgers went pro in 2005. In his first pre-season[2] game, Rodgers completed two out of seven passes and was sacked twice. He did not do much better in other pre-season games. Once the regular season started, Rodgers played very little, as he was the backup to legendary quarterback Brett Favre. However, he gained valuable experience running the scout team[3] and watching Favre.

---

[2] Pre-season games do not count toward a team's win-loss record. They are essentially practice games in which teams have a chance to try out players, give young players experience, and get the team in sync for the regular season.

[3] He helped the defense prepare for their upcoming opponent by mimicking the play the opponents' quarterback.

Box 4.2

The following season, Rodgers felt much more prepared to be an NFL quarterback. He said, "Now, the game is slowing down for me. Although we play at a high speed, you get in game situations and it becomes slow-motion almost. You're able to see things and just react, not think so much" (Wilde, 2006). By "see things," Rodgers means he was able to immediately recognize patterns and react to those patterns. This is in contrast to seeing a field full of individual players moving independently. A quarterback has no time to process the movements of a number of individuals. Pattern recognition becomes essential.

In his popular book *Thinking, Fast and Slow*, Kahneman (2011) proposed two types of thinking systems: System 1, which is fast, intuitive and automatic; and System 2, which is slow, deliberate, and logical. As the quarterback gains experience, he shifts from System 2 thinking (analyzing the position and movements of individual opposing players) to System 1 thinking (sensing patterns and immediately responding). The game only appears to slow down because the processing speeds up.

Truly great quarterbacks are not defined solely by their athletic ability, but by their ability to engage in productive System 1 thinking. Rodgers turned out to be one of these. Once Favre retired, Rodgers took over and enjoyed immediate success, culminating in a Super Bowl championship in 2011.

Unfortunately, school learning often is like seeing a bunch of dots instead of seeing the picture. This bears repeating because it is so fundamental to the struggles of our students. *School learning is like seeing a bunch of dots instead of seeing the picture.* Teachers often cover a wealth of information that is only loosely connected, and students focus on simply memorizing terms and definitions. For learning to be efficient and effective, students need to see the patterns in the information. In the implications section, I discuss ways to support this.

Compared to novices, experts not only perceive more patterns, they perceive more powerful patterns. Novices perceive surface-level patterns whereas experts perceive deeper-level patterns. Try the activity in Box 4.2. Four animals are displayed. One of these animals is not like the others (cue Sesame Street music). Which one is it?

There is not a right or wrong answer to this question. You could say the Polar bear (upper left) is different because it has legs and does not live in the water. You could say the sockeye salmon (bottom left) is different because it is a fish instead of a mammal. You could say the dolphin (upper right) is different because it is a tropical species and the others are arctic species. Or, like my four-year-old daughter, you could say the beluga whale (bottom right) is different because it is smiling. Any of these answers are correct, but some are based on surface-level patterns and others on deep-level patterns.

Surface-level patterns are more immediately observable and obvious, such as the bear having legs. Deep-level patterns are based on higher-level concepts and the differences are not immediately observable, such as the fish not being a mammal or the dolphin not being an arctic species. Deep-level patterns are far more powerful cognitive tools because they are more extensive and generalizable. For example, the concept of *mammals* is an extensive pattern of information that can be used to organize a wealth of information—indeed a far more powerful organization tool than the surface-level pattern of some animals having legs and others fins. This organization creates a more extensive pattern that supports storage and retrieval.

Deep-level patterns also facilitate problem solving. In another famous novice-expert study, Chi, Feltovich, and Glaser (1981) examined the way physics experts (advanced PhD students) and novices (undergraduates) approached physics problems by having them sort problems into groups and explain their groupings. The novices created groups based on surface features. For example, they grouped together problems involving blocks on an inclined plane. The experts, in contrast, created groups based on deep-level features, such as the principles of physics useful for solving the problems. For example, they grouped together problems that could be solved using the principle of conservation of energy.

Novice physics students often struggle because the surface-level patterns they see are not very useful and can even be counterproductive. A student may see a problem and think, "Oh, this is another inclined plane problem. Last time we used Newton's second law, so I need to start by…" However, Newton's second law may be the wrong physics principle for solving the problem, so the student is headed down the wrong path. Physics experts, on the other hand, see deep-level patterns. They see problems in terms of physics principles and thus make sense of problems in a way that facilitates their solution.

The Importance of Meaning and Emotion

In addition to connections, patterns and structure, meaning and emotion are important features of effective memory networks. Take the case of Henry Molaison. As discussed in chapter 3, Henry suffered severe memory disruption after brain surgery to alleviate epileptic seizures. According to Corkin (2013), Henry was unable to recall details of life events with two exceptions: his first flight and his first cigarette. Both of these events were emotionally charged.

As a young 13-year-old boy in 1939, Henry had the magical experience of sitting in the cockpit of single engine plane, feeling the plane shudder down the runway as it gained speed, and then watching the ground drop away as the little plane soared into the sky. To a youth in 1939, such an experience was extraordinary. On separate occasions, Henry recounted vivid details such as the plane's green interior, the feel of the yoke, and the view of the city from above. Henry's first cigarette was also a thrilling experience but in a different way. He commented, "I can remember the first cigarette I ever smoked. It was Chesterfield; I took it from my father's cigarettes. I took one mouthful, and did I cough! You should have heard me" (Corkin, 2013, p. 225).

Despite Henry's extensive memory disruption, the emotional character of these experiences allowed them to be retained and recalled. You can probably relate. Nearly all of us have highly emotional experiences that are seared into our memories. We cannot forget them even if we wanted.

Imagine if, in addition to PageRank, Google calculated EmotionRank for each page. The more emotionally significant a page, the more likely it would be to show up near the top of the search results. This is how your brain works. A part of your brain (primarily the amygdala) registers your emotional response to information and, in a sense, marks highly emotional information for easy recall.

Consider the following research. Canli, Zhao, Brewer, Gabrieli, and Cahill (2000) invited subjects into a lab and had them view 96 pictures ranging in emotional intensity. Participants ranked each picture on a scale of 0 (not emotionally intense at all) to 3 (extremely emotionally intense). Three weeks later, participants were brought back to the lab and given an unexpected recognition test. This test consisted of viewing the 96 original pictures with 48 new pictures mixed in. For each picture, participants were asked to state whether they remembered the pictured or found it familiar.

Consistent with the idea of an EmotionRank function for the brain, those pictures ranked as "extremely emotionally intense" were remembered or recognized as familiar significantly more than the other pictures. Moreover, participant ratings of emotional intensity correlated strongly with activation of the amygdala, and amygdala activation correlated strongly with memory at the upper level of emotional intensity. Simply put, the highly emotional pictures activated the amygdala, making the pictures more memorable.

Classroom research indicates not just "extremely emotionally intense" information is more memorable. Information is also more memorable when associated with commonplace emotions such as meaning and interest (Hidi, 1990). For example, individuals comprehend and recall more from texts written to be interesting (Hidi & Anderson, 1992). They also recall more details and main ideas from texts when interested in the topic (Schiefele & Krapp, 1996).

To summarize, for us to be successful at retaining and retrieving information, the information needs to be part of a network. This network needs to be richly connected, it needs to have a pattern and structure, and it needs to be emotionally significant. In the implications, I discuss ways of supporting the construction of such a network.

IMPLICATIONS

A lot can be written on how to support the construction of effective knowledge networks. I cannot cover everything but will focus on four implications: (1) support connected learning, (2) emphasize depth over memorization, (3) make learning meaningful, and (4) be your own coach.

Support Connected Learning

In college I took a two-semester history of civilization course. This course was taught collaboratively by a humanities professor, a physics professor, and a psychology professor. As we moved through history, we studied interactions between historic events, scientific discoveries, art movements, literary works, philosophies, and so on. For example, we studied deterministic philosophies and considered how such philosophies intersected with behaviorist psychology and Newtonian physics. Later, we studied Einstein's theory of relativity in conjunction with Picasso's cubism. Everything was learned in connection with ideas from other fields. It was one of my favorite college courses and definitely one in which the learning stuck with me. I remember a wealth of content and ideas from that course. Other courses I cannot even remember taking. Seriously, I would need to look at a transcript to recall many of the courses I took in college.

The history of civilization course I described is an example of an integrated curriculum. Integrated curriculums help students build connected networks by interweaving ideas across subject areas. Consequently, they support enduring learning. Unfortunately, integrated curriculums are used infrequently outside of elementary education because teachers do not have expertise across subject areas, and it is difficult to coordinate instruction across multiple teachers. However, teachers can often apply principles of an integrated curriculum within a single-subject course by interweaving ideas across different units. Instead of making each unit its own silo of knowledge, teachers can help students build connections between the knowledge. One approach to achieving such connections is to use crosscutting themes. That is, identify themes common to the main ideas from different units. Chapter 8 provides more details on this strategy.

Students can facilitate their own connected learning through such strategies as elaboration, interleaving, and mnemonics. Elaboration is adding meaningful information to content being learned. For example, instead of just memorizing "society and class" as one of the themes of *Great Expectations*, a student could find multiple examples of this theme in the book, relate these examples to popular films, and consider his or her own experience with popularity and unpopularity. Such elaboration creates a rich network that will support an enduring memory of *Great Expectations* and its "society and class" theme. Elaboration is a way of doing deliberately what Kim Peek did intuitively. Chapter 8 presents information on a specific elaboration strategy referred to as "crisscrossing the landscape."

In their book *Make It Stick*, Brown, Roediger, and McDaniel (2014) emphasize the value of interleaving as a study strategy for effective learning. Interleaving means to intersperse or alternate two things. For example, interspersing blank note-taking pages between the regular pages of a book is interleaving. The *Myth-Busters* TV show team once interleaved the pages of two phonebooks and then tried to pull them apart. Remarkably, it took two *tanks* to pull the phonebooks apart![4] That is not a bad metaphor for appreciating the strength that interleaving provides to learning.

As a study strategy, interleaving means to intersperse or alternate the study of two things. In a study by Kornell and Bjork (2008), participants were asked to study artists in two different ways. In the first way (massed studying), they studied the works of six artists, one artist at a time. Thus, they were given time to study a set of paintings by artist one, then they studied a set by artist two, and so on. In the other method (interleaved studying), they studied the works of six additional artists by alternately viewing paintings from all six artists.

After a distractor task, participants were shown unfamiliar paintings by the same 12 artists and asked to identify the artist. Participants did almost twice as well identifying artists that were studied using the interleaving method versus massed studying. Interestingly, when asked whether massed or interleaving was a more effective study strategy, without being shown the results, 78% of the participants said they believed that massed studying was more effective. We are often unaware of which study strategies maximize our learning.

As evidence that interleaving contributes to enduring memory, Rohrer and Taylor (2007) found that college students who used the interleaving method to practice finding the volume of obscure geometric solids were more successful at solving volume problems a week later than those who used massed practice. Those using interleaving solved 63% of the problems correctly compared to only

---

[4] You can see the episode here: https://www.youtube.com/watch?v=QMW_uYWwHWQ.

20% for those using massed practice—despite the fact that those using massed practice did better during the practice phase.

From an Information Processing perspective, interleaving works because it helps create a more integrated network of knowledge. Different pieces of knowledge are learned in connection with other pieces of knowledge. Chapter 8 discusses the use of crosscutting themes, which is an advanced strategy for interleaving content.

Mnemonics are specific memory strategies used to connect information so it can be better retained in memory. Essentially, they are formal strategies for building a network out of more isolated information. You are likely familiar with a number of mnemonic strategies such as the word mnemonic. For this mnemonic, you take the first letter in a set of words or phrases and make a word out of those letters. For example, to remember the names of the Great Lakes you can take the first letter from Huron, Ontario, Michigan, Erie, and Superior to make the word HOMES. The word HOMES then become a cue to recalling the names of the lakes. It is a simple network but an effective one.

My favorite mnemonic is the memory palace, also known as the method of loci. Perhaps you have seen the BBC *Sherlock* series in which the brilliant Sherlock puts his fingers to his temples, closes his eyes, and mentally goes into his memory palace to search for clues. You too can search your memory palace! Only it does not work quite like it does in the TV series.

To use the memory palace mnemonic, do what Luria's subject, Mr. S., did: first choose a familiar location to be your memory palace. It can be your house, your favorite hiking trail, the local mall—any place that you can picture well in your mind. Then, take a list of items to memorize and place them or something associated with them throughout the location. In line with what we know about memory and emotion, it helps to add emotional drama to the scene.

For example, say I needed to remember the countries of South America. I could use my house as my memory palace. To remember Paraguay, I could place my son on the roof with a paraglider made out of a sheet and he is just about to try paragliding from the roof to the trampoline (he would actually try this). The word "paraglider" will cue my memory of Paraguay, and my anxiety at the image will help fix the memory. Next to my son, I could place Harry Potter saying, "Ur... guys, I think I'll use my Firebolt instead." This will cue my memory for Uruguay. To remember Chile, I place my daughter in her room wrapped up in five blankets because the window is jammed open, snow is blowing in, and icicles are forming on the ceiling. In the kitchen is a bovine (cow) waiting to be milked to help me remember Bolivia. On the counter next to the bovine is a pear covered in maggots. My youngest daughter is riding the bovine dressed as a princess, pointing at the pear, and saying, "Ewwww." This helps me remember Peru.

I continue on this way until I have placed something associated with each country somewhere in or on my house. I continue to focus on creating bizarre, emotional, or humorous situations. Then, when it is time to recall the countries, I visually walk through my memory palace. I walk in my front door, look left, and see my daughter freezing in her room (Chile!). I continue into the kitchen and see my youngest daughter sitting the bovine (Bolivia!) pointing at the pear, saying, "Oooo" (Peru!). Then I walk out the back door and see my son with the paraglider (Paraguay!) and Harry Potter saying, "Ur...guys" (Uruguay!). And so on until I have recalled all the countries.

For Mr. S., the memory palace mnemonic worked to perfection because the images he created this way were permanent. You and I are not so lucky, but we can certainly improve our memory by using the memory palace and other mnemonics. Memory champions do this. Yes, there are world memory champions, and they compete in world memory championships. These individuals are not born with superhero memory powers like Kim Peek and Mr. S. Rather; they are people with ordinary memories who develop elaborate mnemonic systems that help them perform amazing memory feats.

Nelson Dellis, for instance, is a 4-time US memory champion who runs memory-training boot camps. Melanie Pinola participated in one of these boot camps in preparation for the 15th annual USA Memory Championship. Such training involved a number of elaborate imaging strategies. Take for example the strategy Dellis taught for memorizing a random deck of cards. Pinola (2012) explained,

> For each of the 52 cards I had to create a person with an action and object. The Jack of Hearts became my husband frying eggs and the object was eggs in a pan. The King of Spades (KS) was Kevin Spacey (which I thought worked out well initials-wise), lighting a cigarette, and the object was a lighter.... The system enables you to memorize three cards at a time quickly. Imagine the person of the first card doing the action of the person on the second card with the object of the person on the third card. (para. 17)

This method is then combined with the memory palace technique such that each person/action/object image is placed in a specific spot in a familiar location. Pinola gave this example, "Flipping three cards up, I saw Audrey Hepburn (Queen of Diamonds) taking a bath (5 of hearts) with a pirate sword (Jack of Spades) on my couch." To recall the cards, mentally walk through the location and view the images. Try it out. You will be amazed at what you are able to remember using elaborate mnemonic strategies.

Emphasize Depth Over Memorization

As stated previously, school learning is often like seeing a bunch of dots instead of seeing the picture. That is, school learning can consist of trying to input a lot of isolated information instead of constructing a coherent network of knowledge. This has particularly been a problem in the United States, where we have emphasized breadth over depth. For example, based on data from the Third International Mathematics and Science Study, Schmidt, McKnight, and Raizen (1997) concluded that U.S. mathematics and science curricula were an "inch deep

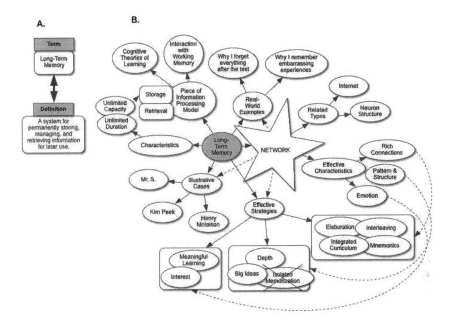

FIGURE 4.1. A. Memorization creates an isolated network consisting of a single connection between pieces of information. B. Development of understanding around big ideas creates a rich network. Note: Image created using *Inspiration®*.

and a mile wide," compared to most other countries. The curricula covered a lot of information (often repeating the same information each year) at a shallow level without a focus on the big ideas and deep-level patterns. Similar accusations were leveled at other U.S. curricula and high school Advanced Placement (AP) courses.

Partially in response to these accusations, the standards movement emphasized defining key ideas in a domain and developing curricula around these ideas. However, the standards have proliferated to such a degree that there is still much debate about whether we have made progress in solving the inch-deep, mile-wide problem (e.g., Li, 2007). Nevertheless, teachers can support learning by making individual efforts to focus on deep understanding of big ideas. A personal example may help illustrate what this means.

When I first started teaching educational psychology courses to pre-service teachers, I did what most teachers do—used the textbook as a basic curriculum guide. Most educational psychology textbooks contain about 15 chapters and are around 700 pages in length. They cover a wealth of information on anything related to learning, learners, development, motivation, instruction, environments, and assessment. Consequently, I found myself quickly moving through topics, and I sensed that I was not adequately helping students get at the meat of the content. Over time, I began to notice core ideas underlying a lot of the content. The metaphors that make up this book are essentially those core ideas.

For example, the textbooks included Piaget, constructivism, conceptual change, critical thinking, problem-based learning, and other related topics in different parts of the book with lots of diverse information about each topic. I realized that nearly all of this information related to single big idea: the mind as an ecosystem (see chapter 6). Hence, I changed my instruction. Instead of teaching these topics separately, I focused on helping my students develop a deep understanding of what it means for the mind to be an ecosystem. When they truly understand this metaphor, they have a holistic "picture" of a certain learning perspective. This picture facilitates retention of information related to this perspective.

Similarly, I focused instruction around the other core metaphors of this book. In doing so, I cut out a lot of specific information because (a) time was needed to develop understanding of the big ideas and (b) students can deduce many of the specifics once they grasp the big idea; that is, once they have a general picture, they can logically fill in a lot of details.

Learners also will benefit tremendously by focusing on depth and big ideas over memorization. Unfortunately, the first study strategy we tend to learn is rehearsal (repeating some information over and over), and many individuals stick with rehearsal as their go-to study strategy even into adulthood (Ormrod, 2011). In many cases, rehearsal takes the form of memorizing terms and definitions. Students make long lists of terms and definitions or flash cards with terms on one side and definitions on the other. Then they dutifully memorize the terms and definitions. This often works just fine for the test, but not so well for long-term retention[5]. You have probably had experiences where you memorized information, aced the test, and then forgot much of what you learned within a few weeks. Why does this happen?

The answer lies in the type of network you create when memorizing versus developing deep understanding of big ideas. Figure 4.1 provides an illustration of the types of networks created through memorization and deep understanding. As shown in part A, memorization of a term ("long-term memory") and its definition creates an isolated network consisting of a single link between the term and definition. Depending on the amount of rehearsing, this link may be relatively strong. Nevertheless, it is still just a single link and the body of information is subject to being lost in the vast expanse of your knowledge. Part B illustrates, to a very limited degree, the type of network created by focusing on understanding—in this case, understanding centered around the big idea associated with long-term memory, which just so happens to be "the network." This more extensive network is far more likely to be retrievable over time.

---

[5] Memorization in the form of rehearsal without elaboration is referred to as *maintenance rehearsal* and generally does not contribute to long-term retention (e.g., Craik & Watkins, 1973).

This is not to imply that memorization is bad. Memorization is often a *necessary* study strategy, but it is *insufficient* for long-term retention when used alone. Think of memorization like physical attraction in a relationship. Physical attraction is often important to a romantic relationship. However, if the relationship is *only* based on physical attraction, then it is unlikely to endure. Enduring relationships are based on things much deeper. Likewise, enduring learning is based on deeper learning strategies.

Make Learning Meaningful

As explained previously, meaningful and emotionally salient information is retained better than other information. Regarding this issue, a lot of valuable advice comes from research on the development and fostering of interest. One of the most common findings is that interest is fostered by establishing relevance (Hidi & Renninger, 2006; Linnenbrink-Garcia, Patall, & Messersmith, 2013).

In a clever study of relevance and interest by Hulleman, Godes, Hendricks, and Harackiewicz (2010), one group of college psychology students was asked to write a letter to someone significant explaining how a topic in the course was relevant to their lives. A second group was asked to find a media report related to the topic and write an essay explaining the relevance of the media report. A third group was asked to write an outlined summary of the topic, and a fourth group was asked to search a database for two abstracts related to the topic and discuss how the abstracts contributed to the topic. The first two groups represented a relevance intervention in that it was theorized students would naturally internalize relevance for the content as a byproduct of writing about its relevance. The second two groups represented a control condition.

As predicted, students in the relevance intervention reported greater interest in the course content at the end of the semester than students in the control condition. The effect was particularly strong for students who had lower prior exam scores. Moreover, the intervention was effective at increasing exam performance for these students with lower prior performance. Simply writing about the relevance of the content increased interest and learning. Chapters 9 and 10 further address the issue of establishing relevance through a presentation of John Dewey's philosophy of education. His philosophy is fundamentally about connecting learning to students' everyday experience.

Active involvement is another strategy commonly found to foster interest (Hidi & Renninger, 2006; Linnenbrink-Garcia et al., 2013). Students frequently find more meaning in the content and develop more interest when provided with opportunities to actively engage the content through hands-on activity, discussion, experimentation, group work, and so on. For example, Mitchel, (1993) found that interest in mathematics was associated with being active participants in the learning process as opposed to listening to lectures.

Box 4.3 summarizes additional strategies effective for fostering interest.

Box 4.3

Bergin (1999) reviewed the research and identified a number of strategies for fostering interest. Some of these are summarized below.

- Novelty – Activities and ideas that are new, different, or unique tend to capture interest.
- Discrepancy – Information in contrast with existing knowledge sometimes triggers interest in resolving the discrepancy.
- A Hole in the Schema – Interest is likely when students discover they are lacking knowledge about something they already know quite a bit about.
- Fantasy – Students often display more interest when the content is embedded in a fantasy context.
- Narrative – Content presented as part of a story is more interesting to students.
- Modeling – Teachers who express enthusiasm for the content help students develop interest in the content.

Note: In order to foster learning, it is best for the interest to be connected to the content. "Seductive details" in text are interesting facts or illustrations disconnected from the main ideas. These seductive details detract from learning as they distract the learner and do not add meaning to the main ideas (Harp & Mayer, 1997).

Be Your Own Coach

Writing about basketball player Draymond Green, Goldberry (2014) wrote that, "You could argue that Green is the 'most improved' player in the NBA this year, but that overlooks a bigger truth: Green is always improving, and the only constant in his game has been its perpetual evolution. He is the best-case scenario for player development in the NBA." This was back in December 2014, before Green helped lead his team to the NBA championship and before his breakout 2015–2016 season in which he made the All-Star team, became one of the NBA's most dominant all-around players, and helped his team break the all-time record with 73 regular season wins.

Green was not expected to be a great NBA player. He was not expected to be an NBA player at all. As a high school player from Saginaw, Michigan, Green was short for his position, not particularly athletic, and overweight. He has since gotten in much better shape, but he still is not notably athletic for an NBA player and is very short for someone who regularly plays power forward and center—Green is 6'7"; most power forwards are at least 6'10" with centers pushing 7.'

Green attended Michigan State University, where he blossomed under hall of fame coach Tom Izzo. Green explained that Coach Izzo "taught me to think the game" (Goldberry, 2014). By "think the game," Green means he learned to anticipate actions, read the tendencies of other teams, be in the right position, make the right play, and so on. As Green was leading his teams to victories in the NCAA tournament, it became a mantra for announcers to comment on his "high basketball IQ."

How did Green develop a high basketball IQ? He was always a smart player, but two factors were critical in helping him capitalize on his potential. First, Green received a lot of one-on-one and team tutoring, not just from Coach Izzo, but the whole coaching staff, including an associate head coach, two assistant coaches, an athletic trainer, a strength and conditioning coach, and others. Green had a knack for appropriating feedback and using it to constantly improve his game. Second, Green took advantage of Michigan State's state-of-the-art video production services. A video production team, consisting of a coordinator and about a dozen student managers, edits and digitizes footage of every game so that players and coaches can efficiently and flexibly review performance. Green spent countless hours with coaches and by himself critiquing his performance and figuring out how to maximize his performance on the court. Green carried this passion for learning from coaches and video feedback to the NBA where it fueled the "perpetual evolution" of his game that made him an all-star.

Students can become all-star learners through the same dedication to learning from feedback on their learning strategies. However, students are at one huge disadvantage compared to Green: they do not have access to an abundance of feedback. There are two good reasons for this. One is resources. Teachers do not have a staff of associate and assistant teachers. Plus, instead of one team of about 13 players, teachers often have multiple "teams" of 20–30 students. Two is the lack of video. You cannot take a video of the learning processes going on in a student's mind and then go back and critique the use of those processes. You cannot have post-performance video sessions in which you directly analyze the degree to which, during the course of a lesson, connections were being made, ideas were being elaborated on, patterns were being constructed, meaning was being sought, and so on. These are largely hidden processes not available for direct observation.

Consequently, to improve as a learner, to become a learning all-star, to be engaged in Draymond Green-like perpetual evolution, a student has to provide feedback to him or herself. That is, the student has to become his or her own coach.

Cognitive psychologists use the term *metacognition* to refer to the process of reflecting on your own thinking (Flavell, 1981). Metacognition is the key to being your own coach and is strongly associated with increased learning (Brown, Bransford, Ferrara, & Campione, 1983). Metacognition involves such things as becoming aware of how the mind processes information and monitoring your own processing. For instance, it involves becoming aware of the nature of long-term memory (which you now are) and monitoring your storage and retrieval processes by making sure you use effective strategies. In this way, you not only process information more effectively, but you learn to learn.

A practical model for becoming your own coach is Zimmerman's (2002) model of self-regulated learning (SRL). Zimmerman divides SRL into three phases: forethought (before the learning activity), performance (during the learning activity), and self-reflection (after the learning activity). In the forethought phase, the individual sets goals and engages in strategic planning (i.e., plans which strategies will be effective). The individual also activates productive motivation patterns, including a belief that one can be a successful learner, an interest in the learning, and a focus on learning as opposed to worrying about grades or the perception of others. This phase is parallel to such coaching actions as preparing a game plan and getting the team focused and energized. During the performance phase, the individual implements the planned strategies, monitors the learning process, makes adjustments as need, and maintains appropriate motivation. This phase is parallel to implementing the game plan, monitoring its effectiveness, making adjustments to counter challenges, and firing up or calming down players as needed. In the self-reflection phase, the individual uses self-evaluation to make judgments about the success of the learning, the effectiveness of the strategies, and the appropriateness of the motivation. These judgments are used to consider improvements for the next learning activity. This last phase is parallel to reviewing game tape, identifying areas of success and areas in need of improvement, and exploring alternative strategies in preparation for the next game.

We tend to believe that successful students are just smarter than the other kids. But this is simply not true. More often, the successful students are successful because they have figured how to be their own coach—often as a result of mentoring by a parent or teacher. One of the great things about Information Processing theory is it can provide everyone with the information needed to be metacognitive. Pair such metacognition with SRL skill development and everyone can be a learning all-star.

REFERENCES

Bergin, D. A. (1999). Influences on classroom interest. *Educational Psychologist*, *34*(2), 87–98. doi:10.1207/s15326985ep3402_2]

Brown, A., Bransford, J., Ferrara, R., & Campione, J. (1983). Learning, remembering, and understanding. In P. H. Mussen (Series Ed.), J. H. Flavell, & E. M. Markman (Eds.), *Handbook of child psychology: Vol. 3. Cognitive development* (pp. 77–166). New York, NY: Wiley.

Brown, P. C., Roediger, H. L., & McDaniel, M. A. (2014). *Make it stick*. Cambridge, MA: Harvard University Press.

Canli, T., Zhao, Z., Brewer, J., Gabrieli, J. D. E., & Cahill, L. (2000). Event-related activation in the human amygdala associates with later memory for individual emotional experience. *Journal of Neuroscience*, *20*(19), RC99.

Chase, W. G., & Simon, H. A. (1973). Perception in chess. *Cognitive Psychology*, *4*, 55–81. doi:10.1016/0010-0285(73)90004-2

Chi, M. T. H., Feltovich, P. J., & Glaser, R. (1981). Categorization and representation of physics problems by experts and novices. *Cognitive Science*, *5*, 121–152. doi:10.1207/s15516709cog0502_2

Corkin, S. (2013). *Permanent present tense: The unforgettable life of the amnesic patient, H.M.* New York: Basic Books.

Craik, F. I. M., & Watkins, M. J. (1973). The role of rehearsal in short-term memory. *Journal of Verbal Learning and Verbal Behavior, 12*, 599–607. doi:10.1016/S0022-5371(73)80039-8

Flavell, J. H. (1981). Cognitive monitoring. In W. P. Dickson (Ed.), *Children's Oral Communication Skills* (pp. 35–60). New York: Academic Press, Inc.

Focus Productions (producer). (2006). *The real rain man* [Television Broadcast]. London, UK.

Goldsberry, K. (2014). *Spartan warrior Draymond Green is the most improved player in the NBA...and he's just getting started.* Grantland. Retrieved from http://grantland.com/the-triangle/spartan-warrior-draymond-green-is-the-most-improved-player-in-the-nba-and-hes-just-getting-started

Harp, S. F., & Mayer, R. E. (1997). The role of interest in learning from scientific text and illustrations: On the distinction between emotional interest and cognitive interest. *Journal of Educational Psychology, 89*, 92–102. doi:10.1037/0022-0663.89.1.92

Hidi, S. (1990). Interest and its contribution as a mental resource for learning. *Review of Educational Research, 60*, 549–571. doi:10.3102/00346543060004549

Hidi, S., & Anderson, V. (1992). Situational interest and its impact on reading and expository writing. In K. A. Renninger, S. Hidi, & A. Krapp (Eds.), *The role of interest in learning and development* (pp. 215–238). Hillsdale, NJ: Erlbaum.

Hidi, S., & Renninger, K. A. (2006). The four-phase model of interest development. *Educational Psychologist, 41*, 111–127. doi:10.1207/s15326985ep4102_4

Hulleman, C. S., Godes, O., Hendricks, B. L., & Harackiewicz, J. M. (2010). Enhancing interest and performance with a utility value intervention. *Journal of Educational Psychology, 102*, 880–895. doi:10.1037/a0019506

Kahneman, D. (2011). *Thinking, fast and slow.* New York: Farrar, Straus and Giroux.

Kornell, N., & Bjork, R. A. (2008). Learning concepts and categories: Is spacing the "enemy of induction"? *Psychological Science, 19*, 585–592. doi:10.1111/j.1467-9280.2008.02127.x

Li, J. (2007). Bridging across the mile-wide and mile-deep chasm: Living and coping with standards-based reform in science education. In D. M. McInerney, S. V. Etten, & M. Dowson (Eds.), *Standards in Education* (pp. 33–57). Charlotte, NC: Information Age Publishing.

Linnenbrink-Garcia, E., Patall, E. A., & Messersmith, E. E. (2013). Antecedents and consequences of situational interest. *British Journal of Educational Psychology, 83*, 591–614. doi:10.1111/j.2044-8279.2012.02080x

Luria, A. R. (1968). *The mind of a mnemonist: A little book about a vast memory.* Cambridge, MA: Harvard University Press.

Mitchell, M. (1993). Situational interest: Its multifaceted structure in the secondary school mathematics classroom. *Journal of Educational Psychology, 85*, 424–436. doi:10.1037/0022-0663.85.3.424

Ormrod, J. E. (2011). *Our minds, our memories: Enhancing thinking and learning at all ages.* Boston, MA: Pearson.

Pinola, M. (2012). How to train your brain and boost your memory like a USA memory champion. Retrieved from http://lifehacker.com/5897708/how-to-train-your-brain-and-boost-your-memory-like-a-usa-memory-champion.

Rohrer, D., & Taylor, K. (2007). The shuffling of mathematics problems improve learning. *Instructional Science, 35*, 481–498. doi:10.1007/s11251-007-9015-8

Schiefele, U., & Krapp, A. (1996). Topic interest and free recall of expository text. *Learning and Individual Differences, 8*, 141–160. doi:10.1016/S1041-6080(96)90030-8

Schmidt, W. H., McKnight, C. C., & Raizen, S. A. (1997). *A splintered vision: An investigation of U.S. mathematics and science education*. Hingham, MA: Kluwer.

Wilde, J. (2006). Rookie no more: A seemingly improved Aaron Rodgers is out to show he's the Packers' future starter. *Madison.com*. Retrieved from http://host.madison.com/sports/rookie-no-more-a-seemingly-improved-aaron-rodgers-is-out/article_4ee3e3de-2e4a-5b29-be19-59be0bfec1b8.html.

Zimmerman, B. J. (2002). Becoming a self-regulated learner: An overview. *Theory into Practice, 41*, 64–70. doi:10.1207/s15430421tip4102_2

PART 3

CONSTRUCTIVISM

Is the mind really like a computer? All metaphors break down, and the *mind as computer* metaphor is no exception. Chapter 5 illustrates how the metaphor breaks down by presenting a story of how a computer would operate if it really were like the human mind. The results are not pretty. Chapter 6 presents an alternative to the computer and network metaphors: *mind as ecosystem*. Together, the *computer as mind* and *mind as ecosystem* metaphors illuminate key principles of a learning perspective known as *constructivism*.

CHAPTER 5

COMPUTER AS MIND

Tanner, an upperclassman in college, went shopping for a new computer. Norbert, an eager salesman, introduced him to the latest and greatest model, the "X–900."

"OK Norbert, what makes the X–900 so amazing?" asked Tanner.

"The GHMLP," answered Norbert confidently.

"The GHM…P, the GHL…M, the what?"

"The GHMLP. Stands for Genuine Human Mind-Like Processor."

"Like a processor based on the actual human mind?" asked Tanner.

"You got it."

"That does sound amazing. I'll take it."

A month later, Tanner was back.

"I want to return this computer," he told Norbert.

"Could you, like, explain what the problem was, sir?"

More like what wasn't the problem, Tanner muttered to himself. Then he took a deep breath and explained.

"OK. What I type on the keyboard should be the same as what shows up on the screen, right? That's the way a normal computer works: I type some words, the same words show up on the screen, life is good, I'm happy. But that's not the way *this* computer works. Oh no. *This* computer has to make things difficult. *This* computer likes to change, distort, alter, modify, and otherwise wreak havoc on what I type in!"

Computers, Cockroaches, and Ecosystems: Understanding Learning through Metaphor, pages 69–83.

After muttering, "Let the customer know you understand his plight" under his breath, Norbert replied, "And this frustrates you?"

"You think?!" exclaimed Tanner.

Norbert glanced around nervously for his manager, who was nowhere to be seen. Norbert looked back at Tanner and asked, "So, um, did the computer always do this?"

"No. Actually it worked just fine out of the box. But then it started to mess around with what I was trying to type in. Just minor things at first. But it got worse over time, and now I never know what is going to happen. At least not exactly."

"Not exactly?"

"Well, I discovered a pattern," said Tanner.

Norbert perked up.

"I've always liked patterns," he said. "Patterns in numbers. Patterns in stars. Patterns in Missy Jorgenson's plaid skirts. She had this blue and green one with thin pink lines and ..." Norbert cut himself off. "So tell me about this pattern."

Tanner stared straight ahead for a good 30 seconds. Then he took another deep breath and explained. "All right. At first I thought the computer just made random changes to what I typed in. But then I had an assignment where I argued both sides of an issue. I choose to write about the environment and first I wrote all about why we need to protect the environment—how it's necessary for sustaining quality of life and all that. Then I tried to write about the other side of the issue, but it wouldn't let me."

"Who?" asked Norbert.

"The computer!"

Norbert looked confused. Tanner shook his head and continued. "It changed everything I wrote to a pro-environment argument. I would write something like, 'We need to put the needs of people ahead of the needs of spotted owls and hump-back chubs' and the computer would display something like, 'We need to put the needs of humans first, and preserving diverse species like the spotted owl and humpback chub is necessary to improving the quality of human life.'"

"Dude, I like that computer," commented a man who was passed by in a tie-dye shirt with a symbol of the earth and the words "Respect Your Mother" on it.

Norbert scrunched his face in a pensive look. "So the pattern is the computer likes what you type in the first time."

"Sort of," replied Tanner. "The pattern is the computer always *reinterprets* what I type based on what I've already typed—even stuff I typed and saved weeks earlier."

"Whoa."

"Watch. If I type 'The sky is blue' then 'The sky is blue' shows up on the screen. So far so good. But now look what happens when I type 'The sky is yellow.'"

Norbert looked at the screen and read, "'The sky is greenish-blue.' Cool!"

"Not cool!" said Tanner, angrily. "I once tried sending my girlfriend an email telling her she is pure and pristine like the sparkling waters of an alpine lake. Only because I had written my issue paper about how our sparkling blue desert reservoirs are really giant mud pits in the making, the computer reinterpreted my typing to say that my girlfriend was like a sparkling lake that looks good on the surface but is a festering mud pit underneath! She's *still* mad at me."

Norbert chuckled, then caught himself and muttered an embarrassed, "Sorry, but is that all? Are there any other problems?"

"Actually, yes," said Tanner emphatically. "Not only does the computer alter what I type in, it changes what I've already saved. When I open an old file, I never know what I'm going to get."

"Is there a pattern to the changes?" asked Norbert.

"Same pattern, but in reverse," responded Tanner. "What I *try* to type in changes what I've *already* typed in. It's a two-way street. I spent hours and hours trying to write things like why we should open up more land to logging and finally I got the computer to accept what I was typing in. Then I opened the previous file and found that the pro-environment argument had been changed to a pro-logging and oil exploration argument! I nearly pulled my hair out!"

Norbert scrunched his forehead, looked around again for the manager, and then spied a worker wheeling a box onto the shop floor. Norbert's eyes lit up. "I've got just the solution for you. What you need is to do is exchange this here X–900 for that X–1000! Not only does it have a Genuine Human Mind-Like Processor, it has a Genuine Human Emotions Chip!"

"Oh great," muttered Tanner.

MAKING SENSE OF THE METAPHOR

This story illustrates a fundamental difference between the human mind and a normal computer. In the constructivist perspective, the human mind is, well, constructive. It interprets, transforms, and imposes meaning on incoming information based on prior knowledge. At the same time, stored information is constantly being transformed and reconstructed based on new knowledge. It works like the X–900.

Here are some humorous examples of such construction in action, taken from actual college student papers (Henriksson, 2001):

- "Members of the upper class were able to live posthumorously [sic] through the arts and facts buried with them." (p. 6)
- "South Africa followed 'Apart Hide,' a policy that separated people by skin color." (p. 129)
- "A position as a lady-in-mating helped a young girl's chances for a marriage." (p. 30)
- "The Civil Rights movement in the USA turned around the corner with Martin Luther Junior's famous 'If I had a Hammer' speech." (p. 130)
- "Joan of Ark was famous as Noah's wife." (p. 10)

- "Judyism was the first monolithic religion. It had one big God named 'Yahoo.'" (p. 9)
- "Socrates was accused of sophmorism [sic] and sentenced to die of hemroyds [sic]." (p. 15)

You laugh, but we have all done this. In fact, all learning involves a degree of transformation, distortion, and reconstruction of meaning. This chapter addresses three key principles of constructivism: (1) there is no pure transfer of meaning from the environment to the mind, (2) there is no pure recall of information from memory, and (3) we draw on our existing ideas to construct new ideas.

The O.J. Trial and the Construction of Meaning

The first principle of constructivism is that there is *no pure transfer of meaning from the environment to the mind*. Sorry, it just doesn't happen. We use our existing knowledge of the world to makes sense of new ideas, new experiences, and new information. Inevitably, this results in unique interpretations or transformations of the new ideas, experiences, and information.

Take our first two college students' responses as examples. The first student was likely unfamiliar with the term "artifact." So, when the instructor lectured about artifacts, he or she made sense of the language in terms of familiar words: arts and facts. The second student also seemed to be struggling to make sense of unfamiliar information. Therefore, instead of hearing "apartheid," he or she processed the information about separation and skin color and came up with "Apart Hide." And since we're on a roll, I should mention the student who referred to the Palestinians as the "Palaced Indians."

Another example of how the mind interprets and transforms information is what I call the teenage drama converter. Benign information from parents such as "Come in for dinner" goes into the teenage brain, runs through the drama converter, and comes out as "Get in here right now you good-for-nothing, lazy bum!" Or a neutral face is run through the drama converter and comes out as the Mel-Gibson-Braveheart-I'm-Going-to-Kill-You face[1].

On a more serious note, consider the reactions of black and whites to the O.J. Simpson verdict. Before Trayvon Martin, before Ferguson, before #blacklivematter and #bluelivesmatter, there was O.J. Simpson and the "trial of the century." O.J. Simpson was a superstar running back for the Buffalo Bills in the 1970s and later became a successful actor and celebrity. On June 12th 1994, O.J.'s ex-wife Nicole Brown and her friend Ronald Goldman were found murdered. On June 17th 1994, the NBA finals and other TV programs were interrupted for a live broadcast of a low-speed police chase of a white Bronco with O.J., the murder suspect, inside.

---

[1] Teenagers are more likely to interpret a neutral face as a hostile or angry face (Siegel, 2013).

Eventually O.J. turned himself in, and his case went to trial in 1995. Everyone tuned in to the trial. Cameras were allowed in the courtroom, so everyone got to see the evidence and hear network experts dissect and analyze every detail. As the trial progressed, opinion polls regarding O.J.'s innocence were regular news fodder. They were often broken down by race, which became a major issue in the trial. O.J. was African American. His ex-wife was white. The Los Angeles Police Department (LAPD), which had jurisdiction in the case, had a history of alleged racial bias.

In the end, O.J. was acquitted, and final polls were conducted. In one CNN/ *Time* poll, 62% of whites reported that they believed O.J. was guilty. Only 14% of blacks believed he was guilty. That is a difference of nearly 50 percentage points! The poll also asked respondents if they believed that O.J. was framed. This was a key issue in the trial because a central claim of the defense was that the detective on the case, Mark Fuhrman, was a racist who had physically abused black suspects and repeatedly used the n-word in reference to blacks. They argued that he planted evidence in an attempt to bring down a prominent black man. In the CNN/ *Time* poll, nearly two-thirds (65%) of blacks, but only a quarter (26%) of whites agreed that O.J. was framed.

What is going on here? Is it simply a matter of racial bias? Are whites prone to accuse O.J. because he is black? Are blacks prone to excuse him for the same reason? While it is tempting to believe this, there is actually a deeper and more interesting story to tell.

Take a moment and think about your associations with police from your youth. If you come from a mainstream middle-class or upper-class background, these associations were likely quite positive. Maybe you participated in Safety City as a young child, and a friendly policeman taught you how to obey street signs and traffic rules. Maybe you got candy from generous policemen at a community parade. Maybe you read Richard Scarry books in which Sergeant Murphy keeps Busytown safe from thieves like Bananas Gorilla. Maybe you got a police station Lego set as a Christmas present. Maybe you dressed up like a policeman for Halloween. Maybe you wanted to be a policeman.

When I was 12, my neighbors asked me to watch their house during a funeral. On one of my rounds checking the house, I noticed a car parked in front. It seemed suspicious, so I walked up and carefully wrote down the license plate number. Soon after, the alarm went off, and a man ran out the front door, jumped in the car, and sped off. I stood dumbfounded and then went home and called the police. A short time later, they showed up and began talking with me about the episode. At one point, a policeman leaned over to a newly arrived officer, smiled, and said something like, "Get this, he walked right up to the car and wrote down the license plate number. We got this guy." Then he told me what a great job I had done. I felt so proud. It was such an honor to be praised by the police. They were the good guys. The heroes.

Certainly not all associations with the police are positive. However, it is common for the police to be portrayed as brave defenders of justice, compassionate servants of the people, fair administrators of the law, and so on. Even as we get older and more cynical, most of us maintain a reasonably positive perception of the police. It is easy to believe that everyone has a perception of the police that involves a degree of trust and respect. Such a belief could not be more wrong.

In 1999, Rod Brunson, Jody Miller and a team of researchers began interviewing young black men living in St. Louis about their experiences with the police and their perceptions of the police (Brunson & Miller, 2006). They deliberately sought out "at-risk" young men because they figured such individuals would have had numerous interactions with the police. By the following year, they had interviewed 40 individuals ranging in age from 13 to 19. All had been involved in some delinquent activities, and 65% had previously been arrested. The accounts provided by these young men and their stated opinions about the police were telling.

Consider the case of Ricky, who was representative of many of the other young men. Ricky described a confrontation that occurred as he was hanging out with his girlfriend after watching a movie. According to Ricky, an officer got into his face, cussing at him, telling him to move. Ricky called the officer an Uncle Tom, and the officer responded by beating him. What upset Ricky was not so much the beating, but that the officer started harassing him for no reason: "I mean, I was dressed real nice. I didn't have on no tennis shoes. I had on some like, khaki pants, a button up shirt. I mean, we was just standin' out there" (p. 630)

Experiences like this led Ricky to believe that the police were always looking to hassle young black men like himself. He explained,

> The police will ride up on a group of guys, they'll get out, they'll make you lay on the ground, they'll pull your clothes all off you. Or they make you take your shoes and socks off…I mean, they know I don't sell dope, they know I go to school everyday…Every time they check me…Check my shoes, make me take my socks off. Man it's cold outside. "Pull your pants down.."..all types of stuff, man, and it's freezin' outside. (p. 624)

Many of the other young men shared similar accounts and expressed similar opinions about the police. They believed the police engaged in intrusive and tormenting behavior just to hassle them. The young men referred to such behavior as "just messin' with us." One of them explained, "They'll just come out and just, they ain't, they wouldn't like lock us up, they just take all us down to the station or whatever, just have us sitting there for hours and then let us go. They'll take your money and stuff, have to walk home" (p. 625).

They also believed that a lot of the *messin'* was race motivated, even when black cops were involved. A young man commented, "I got white friends and stuff and [the police] don't really do nuttin' to them. They sell drugs and everything just like everybody else do" (p. 634). Another young man recounted being pulled over when he was riding in a car driven by a white lady. Instead of approaching the driver, the cops approached him: "I'm like, 'this don't make no sense…why they ain't pull her out, asking for her driver's license and stuff?' But they pulled me out and asking [for] my ID and stuff. You know, I couldn't understand it" (p. 633–634).

In addition, the young men believed many of the officers were corrupt. One young man explained, "If you ain't got no proof of where your money coming from, then they automatically suspect that it's drug money and they take as much as you got…That's messed up" (p. 631).

The attitude of these young black men living in St. Louis is perhaps best summed up by these words from Ricky:

> I mean, we know how they gonna treat us when they come up. So usually when we see 'em we run. We already know what they gonna do…It's just how they treat people, you know. They treat you like, over there, like you not even human. (p. 631)

"We know how they gonna treat us." "When we see 'em we run." That's the perception of the police. That's the attitude: *If you see a cop, you run. It doesn't matter if you're innocent. It doesn't matter if you're dressed nice. The cop's going to mess with you anyway. You see a cop, you just run.*

Brunson and Miller (2006) argue that elevated mistrust of the police by minorities is one of the most consistent findings in the research on perceptions of the police. Polls back this up. A 1999 gallop poll asked respondents, "Do you have a favorable or unfavorable opinion of your local police?" Eighty–five percent of whites stated they had a favorable opinion but only 58% of blacks reported a favorable opinion.

A 1999 Harris poll posed the question, "Do you think the police in your community treat all races fairly or do they tend to treat one or more of these groups unfairly?" Among whites, 67% said they believed the police treated all races fairly, and just 25% said one or more races were treated unfairly. The results were flipped for blacks. Only 30% said the police treated all races fairly, and 63% said the police treated one or more race unfairly. A second question asked, "Are you sometimes afraid that the police will stop and arrest you when you are completely innocent, or not?" A mere 16% of whites said yes, but nearly half (43%) of blacks said yes.

These opinions, beliefs, and experiences comprise a conceptual framework for interpreting information that involves the police. That is, people make sense of police-related events in terms of their existing conceptual framework about the police. Now we can understand the reactions to the O.J. trial (and related events such as Ferguson). If your framework involves positive interactions with the police and you generally believe that the police are fair, then the police conspiracy argument in the O.J. case do not make a lot of sense, and you are likely to interpret the evidence in ways that fit with O.J. being guilty rather than the LAPD being dirty.

On the other hand, if your experience is that of being disrespected by the police, pulled over for no reason, stripped down and searched, relieved of your money; and your attitude toward the police is summed up by the phrase "We know how they gonna treat us…when we see 'em we run," then is it really so hard to believe in a police conspiracy? Is it really so hard to accept that a detective who used the n-word might plant evidence just to bring down a prominent black man? I think not.

Likewise, when learning in the classroom or elsewhere, we tend to make sense of new information in terms of our existing conceptual frameworks. We put details and ideas together in ways that make sense with our existing ideas, beliefs, and experiences. This point cannot be over-emphasized. As learners, we don't see reality as it is. There is no pure transfer of meaning from the instructor or the environment to the mind. Instead, we *construct* a reality. We *construct* meaning. And we do so based on our existing ideas, beliefs, and experiences.

An Ironic Accusation and the Reconstruction of Memory

The second principle of constructivism is that there is *no pure recall of information from memory*. Every time we recall information, we distort, transform, and reinterpret the information. In fact, the whole idea that we have memories and information "stored" in a long-term memory where they remain unchanged is challenged by constructivism. Instead of a static long-term memory like that of a computer hard drive, constructivism proposes the mind is comprised of memory traces.

When we recall a memory, we recall a number of memory traces and then fill in the gaps with information that makes sense or has some association to the memory traces. Thus, memories often change because (a) we recall different memory traces and (b) we fill them in with different information. Memory traces do not have to come from the same event or learning episode. In fact, we often unknowingly combine memory traces from different events or learning episodes. We also unknowingly create new memory traces as we combine them and fill in the gaps.

Baddeley (2004) recorded an incredibly ironic example of memory reconstruction involving the Australian eyewitness testimony expert Donald Thompson. Based on his own research and that of many others, Thompson was convinced that eyewitness testimonies are not the bastions of reliability we think them to be. He argued that eyewitnesses are easily influenced by many forms of bias and often distort events, falsely recall details, or confuse observations.

On one occasion, Thompson participated in a live TV discussion about the unreliability of eyewitness testimonies. He appeared with an official of the Australian Civil Rights Committee and an assistant police commissioner. A short time later, Thompson was arrested on rape charges. He was placed in a lineup and positively identified by the victim. Upon learning details of the case, Thompson realized the reported time of the rape was the same as his live TV discussion. He said he could not have committed the rape because he was participating in the live TV discussion and had the civil rights official and an assistant police commissioner to confirm his alibi, not to mention the whole TV audience.

So what is going on here? On the one hand, you have a defendant with a seemingly airtight alibi. On the other hand, you have a victim positively identifying Thompson. Further, there was no reason to question the sincerity of the victim, who had no motive for falsely accusing Thompson.

The policeman taking Thompson's statement sided with the victim. In response to Thompson's claim to have such prominent and numerous witnesses to his alibi, the policeman sarcastically replied, "Yes, and I suppose you've got Jesus Christ, and the Queen of England too."

However, further investigation revealed a startling fact. The victim was watching TV at the time of the attack. In fact, she was watching the very program on which Thompson appeared. Suddenly, the pieces fell together. The victim *had* seen Thompson at the time of the rape. His face was encoded as a memory trace, along with other memory traces that comprised this horrific experience. Later, when the victim recalled the traumatic experience, the memory trace of Thompson's face was recalled as the face of the actual rapist. For the victim, Thompson as the rapist was a real memory. But this memory, like all memories, was distorted. There is no pure recall of information from memory.

To understand just how pervasive memory reconstruction is, try playing this game. Get together with a group of friends or relatives, choose some event from the past that all of you experienced, and have everyone write down their memory of the event with as much detail as possible. Now the fun part. Compare your memories. You will often be surprised at just how different your memories are. Most likely, you remember your actions in a far more positive light than the others do!

The fact that memories are distorted does not mean that all your memories are total fabrications. The point is that our memories are imperfect reconstructions. This same point applies to our memories of learned information. The mind is not like a file cabinet where all the information about a topic is stored in a file, and we recall the information by pulling out the complete file and reading off the information verbatim. Instead, the information exists as memory traces. When we recall our knowledge of a particular topic, we reconstruct our understanding by selecting memory traces and filling in the gaps.

As with our experiential memories, we often confuse memory traces. This seems to be what was going on with the college student who wrote that "Martin Luther Junior" gave a famous speech titled "If I had a Hammer." For those of you unfamiliar with the '60s, "If I Had a Hammer" was a famous Pete Seeger song popularized by Peter, Paul, and Mary (King's speech was titled "I Have a Dream"—you knew that one, right?).

We also distort our knowledge as we fill in the gaps. This was likely the case with the student who said Judyism had one big god named Yahoo. He likely had fuzzy memory traces of the terms Judaism and Yahweh or Yehova (which were used as names for God in Judaism) and filled in the gaps with other information: *Let's see. The name of their god was something like Yea, Ya, Yaho...Yahoo! That's it!* Either that or he was a she named Judy who really wanted to found her own religion and was awed by the apparent omniscience of the Internet.

In the constructivist perspective, the mind is not a computer hard drive. There is no pure recall of information. Instead, the mind is a constructor of meaning based on memory traces. This may seem problematic, but it is actually quite important, as it allows us to effectively deal with ambiguous and incomplete information[2]. It also allows us to do something profoundly human: come up with new ideas.

A Rocking Dog and New Ideas Out of Old

The third principle of constructivism is that *we draw on our existing ideas to construct new ideas.* One of the great benefits of having a constructive mind is that we can construct new ideas. Computers, as great as they are, just cannot construct ideas the way humans construct ideas. When it comes to creativity, we leave computers in the dust (go humans!).

The capacity to develop new ideas based on existing ideas if often best illustrated by kids. There are endless examples of such kid construction. I will share a few examples from my own kids, who I often brought into my education classes so we could observe their theories about such things as the cause of the seasons and weather, why leaves change color and fall, why we don't fall off the bottom of the earth and so on.

When my oldest daughter, McKinley, was seven, she developed the idea that trees hold onto the leaves during the summer. But when the fall comes, the trees start to go to sleep and as they go to sleep, they cannot hold onto the leaves anymore so they drop them. When my son, Hayden, was about the same age, he explained that we don't fall off the bottom of the earth because gravity is like a "little suction thing" that keeps us on the earth.

Once I made a video of their theories. I asked my daughter Kaya (then four years old) what makes wind. She responded, "The treeees. Because they blow." Then she started shaking her hand. "Because they shake their selves."

"And that makes the wind?" I asked.

"Yeah. Because when they get too tall, they shake."

These examples are similar to the memory reconstruction examples, but there is a bit more going on. My kids are not just confusing or combining memory traces, they are using memory traces in a creative way to conceive new ideas. This ability to create new ideas is uniquely human. Computers just cannot do it the same way. Consider this song that Kaya came up with at the end of the video (to the tune of *Hush, Little Baby*):

---

[2] For example, it is very difficult to program a computer to interpret verbal language because verbal language is so inconsistent and incomplete. But we learn to do this effortlessly at a young age. In fact, we mk sns of lnguag evn wn lts of inf is mssng or enev wehn the wrods are slepled otu of odrer!

If that—Mama will buy you a rocking dog.
If that rocking dog won't bark,
Mommy will buy you a flower.
If that flower doesn't smell,
I'll give you just some scent.
And if it doesn't—And if it still be little rocks,
It still will be ok.

How do you get a computer to come up with the idea of a rocking dog that won't bark? I am sure some computer scientist could write a complex program that adds additional random verses to the song. But that is the point. The computer requires a program that specifically *tells* it what do to achieve a specified outcome. We do it naturally without a predetermined program and outcome. We create. And, perhaps, that is the best description of learning from a constructivist perspective. We create.

IMPLICATIONS

Knowledge Cannot Be Directly Transmitted

A lot of teaching and learning perspectives are based on a transmission metaphor: the teacher or textbook is like a radio transmitter sending out a signal. If the signal is strong and the individual is tuned in, then the signal will be received as broadcast. Learning failures occur when only part of the signal is received due to a weak signal or a tuned out student.

From the constructivist perspective, such a metaphor is preposterous. No matter how strong the signal or how tuned in the individual, there can be no direct transmission of a message. The individual is always constructing his or her own unique understanding of the incoming information. A teacher may be broadcasting Bach, but one student may be hearing Beethoven, another Mozart, and a third Lady Gaga. Ok, that last one is a stretch and the transformation is not always that dramatic, but the point is, there is always *some* transformation.

Different folks have different ideas about how to deal with this transformation problem, and whether we should think of it as a problem at all. Some people suggest that because the mind will creatively reconstruct information, instructors should be extremely clear, and constantly reiterate key points. The hope is that clarity and repetition will reduce the amount of faulty knowledge construction.

Others argue that instructors should focus more on the learner than the message. They argue it is a given that learners are going to construct unique understandings, so instructors need to become more aware of these individual understandings and build on them (Smith, diSessa, & Roschelle, 1993). That is, instructors need to constantly get feedback about how individual learners are making sense of the new information. For example, instructors can probe students' understandings during the course of a lesson or unit, use formative assessments, have students discuss and share ideas about the content, and so on. By getting such feedback, instructors can aid and guide the knowledge construction process.

Still others argue that instructors should take advantage of the mind's creative capacity and give individuals a more active role in their learning. Why not make knowledge construction the focus of learning, since the mind is always involved in a process of reconstruction anyway? That is, instead of lecturing and passing out closed-ended worksheets, why not let students discover new ideas, problem solve, experiment, and so on? The belief is that individuals do a better job of constructing an understanding when they do so deliberately in the role of a knowledge constructor rather than unintentionally in the role of a knowledge receiver (Ball, 1992; Brown & Campione, 1994; Duckworth, 1987).

Most educators who identify with a constructivist perspective advocate this type of discovery learning. However, they also emphasize the need for structure and scaffolding found in such instructional models as problem-based learning (PBL) (Savin-Baden & Major, 2004). Thus, instead of leaving students to discover on their own, teachers will organize a set of tasks to guide the discovery process, identify appropriate resources, work with students to set goals, push students to explain thinking, meet with groups regularly to discuss progress, provide direct instruction and expert guidance as needed, and so on (Hmelo-Silver, Duncan, & Chinn, 2007).

I created a PBL project for an education course because I decided I was a hypocrite for teaching constructivism without giving my students the full constructivist experience. For this project, I have my students learn about student motivation by solving the motivation problems of Calvin from the *Calvin and Hobbes* comics[3]. Calvin is a great subject of study because has all the classic motivation problems—learned helplessness, self-handicapping, utter boredom in school despite a love for learning and discovery out of school, and so on. I place students in groups and each group selects a motivation theory, which they research with the aid of activities and resources. Then they create a wiki (like a website) that describes their theory and use it to explain Calvin's motivation problems, identify the cause of those problems, and propose solutions. I meet with the groups each class period to discuss their understanding of the theory, its application to Calvin, and progress on the wiki. Students submit a draft of their wiki and receive feedback from me and two other groups, after which they revise and create a final product. Finally, I do a jigsaw activity in which I create new groups consisting of an "expert" in each motivation theory and, together, they write a letter to Ms. Wormwood (Calvin's teacher) with advice on how to address all of Calvin's motivation problems.

Thus, my students are learning about motivation through their own active investigation, but there is a lot of structure and scaffolding built in, so they do not feel too lost and frustrated. Although, it is fair to say, some students do feel lost and nearly all students feel frustration at some point. PBL is a more demanding

---

[3] You can view the project here: http://calvinproject.wikispaces.com.

learning model than traditional instruction. But there is a payoff. As mentioned in chapter 2, students who learn content through PBL display a deeper level of learning, particularly an enhanced ability to apply learning in a real world context (Dochey, Segers, Van de Bossche, & Gijbels, 2003; Hung, Jonassen, & Liu, 2008). I found this to be true of my own project. Compared to students who learned about motivation theory through lecture, discussion, and small group activities, those who did the PBL project performed nearly twice as well on a task requiring application of motivation theory to real-world scenarios (Bergstrom, Pugh, Phillips, & Machlev, 2016).

We See and Make Sense of the World Differently

You already knew this, but you may not have understood why we see the world so differently. Other people do not disagree with you simply because they are stubborn or mentally deficient. They disagree with you because they have different conceptual frameworks. They are making sense of the world the best they can given their existing ideas and experiences. Unless they are teenagers, that is. Then none of the above applies.

Where does this leave us? On the one hand, we might choose to give up the idea that we are all going to see the world in the same way. Our conceptual frameworks for making sense of the world are just too different. This may be either depressing or liberating. Depressing, because (a) you now have confirmation that nobody understands you and (b) your hopes for world peace probably just took a hit. Liberating, because you now do not have to get so angry with people who have a different political, cultural, or religious opinion—which may just lead to world peace (good, we got that hope restored).

On the other hand, we may focus on the fact that we can better understand the perspectives of others by understanding their conceptual frameworks. That is, we can seek to understand the set of ideas and experiences they use to make sense of the world in particular situations. And such understanding may, once again, lead to world peace (that's two for world peace and only one against—I'm feeling better).

Knowing that we see and make sense of the world differently also has important implications for learning. As teachers, we can understand that our students are not misinterpreting information because they are stubborn or dumb. Often it is because they are using different conceptual frameworks to make sense of the information. By understanding their conceptual frameworks, we can better understand them and work toward a common understanding.

As learners, we can understand that our own perceptions may not be The Truth. A healthy sense of skepticism about the certainty of our own knowledge goes a long way to developing every more accurate perceptions. Of course this assertion assumes that an objective reality actually exists, which may not be the case if we take constructivism seriously. Let us explore this possibility.

Does an Objective Reality Exist?

If we all see and make sense of the world differently because we always transform incoming information and reconstruct existing knowledge, then is there any hope for an objective view of the world? Can we even be sure that an objective reality exists? What does this mean for Truth? Can we know anything with certainty?

If we took constructivism seriously, not just sort of seriously but seriously seriously, then we might end up like the ruler of the universe in Douglas Adams' *Hitchhiker's Guide to the Galaxy* (2002) series. Here is a passage describing the ruler of the universe talking to his cat from *The Restaurant at the End of the Universe*:

> "Pussy not eat his fish, pussy get thin and waste away, I think," said the man. Doubt crept into his voice.
>
> "I imagine this is what will happen," he said, "but how can I tell?"…
>
> "I think fish is nice, but then I think rain is wet, so who am I to judge?"
>
> He left the fish on the floor for the cat, and retired to his seat.
>
> "Ah, I seem to see you eating it," he said at last, as the cat exhausted the entertainment possibilities of the speck of dust and pounced onto the fish.
>
> "I like it when I see you eat fish," said the man, "because in my mind you will waste away if you don't."…
>
> "Fish come from far away," he said, "or so I'm told. Or so I imagine I'm told. When the men come, or when in my mind the men come in their six black shiny ships, do they come in your mind too? What do you see, pussy?"
>
> He looked at the cat, which was more concerned with getting the fish down as rapidly as possible than it was with these speculations.
>
> "And when I hear their questions, do you hear questions? What do their voices mean to you? Perhaps you just think they're singing songs to you." He reflected on this, and saw the flaw in the supposition.
>
> "Perhaps they are singing songs to you," he said, "and I just think they're asking me questions."…
>
> "I think I must be right in thinking they ask me questions," he said. "To come all the way and leave all these things just for the privilege of singing songs to you would be very strange behavior. Or so it seems to me. Who can tell, who can tell." (pp. 279–281)

Is the ruler of the universe crazy or is he simply willing to do what none of us has the courage to do: live life as if the only certain truth is that we cannot be certain of any truth? Personally, I think he's crazy, but who can tell, who can tell?

REFERENCES

Adams, D. (2002). *The ultimate hitchhiker's guide to the galaxy.* New York, NY: Ballantine Books.

Baddeley, A. (2004). *Your memory: A user's guide.* Buffalo, NY: Firefly Books.

Ball, D. L. (1992). Halves, pieces, and twoths: Constructing and using representational contexts in teaching fractions. In T. P. Carpenter, E. Fennema, & T. A. Romberg (Eds.), *Rational numbers: An integration of research* (pp. 157–195). Hillsdale, NJ: Erlbaum.

Bergstrom, C., Pugh, K. J., Phillips, M., & Machlev, M. (2016). Effects of problem-based learning on recognition learning and transfer accounting for GPA and goal orientation. *Journal of Experimental Education, 00,* 1–23. doi:10.1080/00220973.2015.1083521

Brown, A. L., & Campione, J. C. (1994). Guided discovery in a community of learners. In K. McGilly (Ed.), *Classroom lessons: Integrating cognitive theory and classroom practice* (pp. 229–270). Cambridge, MA: MIT Press/Bradford Books.

Brunson, R. K., & Miller, J. (2006). Young black men and urban policing in the united states. *British Journal of Criminology, 46,* 613–640. doi:10.1093/bjc/azi093

Dochy, F., Segers, M., Van de Bossche, P., & Gijbels, D. (2003). Effects of problem-based learning: A meta-analysis. *Learning and Instruction, 13,* 533–568. doi:10.1016/S0959-4752(02)00025-7

Duckworth, E. (1987). *The having of wonderful ideas.* New York, NY: Teachers College Press.

Henriksson, A. (2001). *Non campus mentis: World history according to college students.* New York, NY: Workman.

Hmelo-Silver, C. E., Duncan, R. G., & Chinn, C. A. (2007). Scaffolding and achievement in problem-based and inquiry learning: A response to Kirschner, Sweller, and Clark (2006). *Educational Psychologist, 42,* 99–107. doi:10.1080/00461520701263368

Hung, W., Jonassen, D., & Liu, R. (2008). Problem-based learning. In J. M. Spector, M. D. Merrill, J. V. Merriënboer, & M. P. Driscoll (Eds.), *Handbook of research on educational communications and technology* (pp. 485–506). New York, NY: Erlbaum.

Savin-Baden, M., & Major, C. H. (2004). *Foundations of problem-based learning.* Maidenhead, UK: Open University Press.

Siegel, D. J. (2013). *Brainstorm: The power and purpose of the teenage brain.* New York, NY: Tarcher.

Smith, J. P., diSessa, A. A., & Roschelle, J. (1993). Misconceptions reconceived: A constructivist analysis of knowledge in transition. *The Journal of the Learning Sciences, 3,* 115–163. doi:10.1207/s15327809jls0302_1

CHAPTER 6

MIND AS ECOSYSTEM

If the mind is not a computer according to the constructivist perspective, then what is it? Influential scholars, such as Jean Piaget, used a *mind as ecosystem* metaphor. A story about Yellowstone National Park describes the changing nature of an ecosystem and serves as a model for the mind-as-ecosystem perspective.

In an article published in *Sporting Classics*, Todd Tanner (2013) wrote:

> Twenty years ago, when I was guiding fly fishermen in [Yellowstone National Park], my clients could hardly wait for the mid-July Yellowstone opener. When the big day finally arrived, we'd load up my truck and drive to Fishing Bridge, where trout by the hundreds—sometimes by the thousands—would put on an incredible show. Then we'd head down to Buffalo Ford, where we'd wade one of the most pristine and picturesque rivers on the planet in our quest for those oversized, incredibly colorful Yellowstone cuts. (p. 65)

Todd and his clients were not alone. Fly fishermen from all over the country used to converge on the Yellowstone River for the July 15th opener. Many would rise before dawn and reach the river just as the first rays of light struck the ever-present blanket of mist rising off the river. There they would spend the morning catching Yellowstone cutthroat trout, whose sides glowed with yellow and orange hues rivaling the glow of the mist being burned off by the morning sun.

Computers, Cockroaches, and Ecosystems: Understanding Learning through Metaphor,
pages 85–106.

The Yellowstone cutthroat trout were prized for both their beauty and abundance. Each spring, thousands of cutthroats migrated out of Yellowstone Lake into the Yellowstone River and surrounding tributaries to spawn. During the spawn, they developed a bright golden color and crimson cheeks. Many fish retained their spawning colors and remained in the river for the opener, and eagerly rose to flies cast by enthralled fishermen. The Yellowstone opener was, to some degree, the fly fisherman's equivalent of golf's Masters tournament. I have been there for the opener. It is one of my cherished fishing memories.

By the mid-2000s, Tanner no longer took clients to the Yellowstone opener. Why? No mass gathering of cutthroat. The Yellowstone River is part of an ecosystem, and in an ecosystem, one small change can have far-reaching effects. In this case, that one small change was the introduction of a few lake trout into Yellowstone Lake.

The Yellowstone cutthroat is the native trout of Yellowstone Lake and the surrounding rivers and tributaries, having migrated to the area after glacial ice receded some 7,000 to 8,000 years ago. In 1994, lake trout were discovered in Yellowstone Lake. Lake trout are not native to the region. They are drab in color and generally not accessible to the fly fisherman because they live at the bottom of deep lakes. However, lake trout get big, which is why some anglers prize them and, presumably, why someone illegally planted them in Yellowstone Lake.

As you might suspect, lake trout get big by eating other fish. In Yellowstone Lake, they start to eat cutthroat at age four. By six or seven years of age, they feed almost exclusively on cutthroats. Researchers have estimated that a mature lake trout will eat an average of 41 cutthroat trout each year (Ruzycki, Beauchamp, & Yule, 2003). This is bad news for the Yellowstone cutthroat. Since 1994, the population has crashed. As of 2010, most estimates put the population at about 10% of historic levels (Licis, 2010). There are additional causes for this population crash (e.g., whirling disease). However, the introduction of lake trout seems to be, by far, the most significant factor.

The lake trout in Yellowstone Lake is a classic example of an *invasive species*, a term biologists use for non-native species that take root in an ecosystem and wreak havoc. As a native species, the Yellowstone cutthroat was important to the ecosystem surrounding Yellowstone Lake. Because the cutthroat often feed near the surface, they were an important food source for surface-feeding eagles, ospreys, and pelicans. When the cutthroats disappeared from the area, so did many birds. Further, epic cutthroat spawning runs numbered in the tens of thousands. As these fish ran up small tributaries each spring, grizzly bears would feast on the protein-rich fish much the way their northern brethren feast on salmon. When the size of these spawning runs plummeted, the bears had to search elsewhere for food, and subsisted on a poorer diet.

Scientists concluded that a remarkable 42 species of birds and mammals fed on the Yellowstone cutthroat (Gresswell, 2009). Now the feeding and migration habits of these species have been disrupted, and these disruptions are affecting still other species. In fact, it is impossible to estimate the full impact of the lake trout on the Yellowstone Lake ecosystem. In an ecosystem, everything is connected and one change can have far-reaching effects.

MAKING SENSE OF THE METAPHOR

Our Conceptual Ecosystem

Although depressing, the Yellowstone Lake example does nicely show how an ecosystem functions. An ecosystem is an interrelated system of plants, animals, microorganisms, and physical environments (e.g., rocks, minerals). Moreover, it is a dynamic, ever-changing system. Change may be slow and gradual or rapid and abrupt, but there is always change. Over time, some organisms become more prominent, others die off, and new variations come into being.

Many learning theorists have come to think about the mind in a similar way. They envision the mind as a *conceptual* ecosystem—an interrelated system of ideas, knowledge, and memories that is always changing and evolving.

The Swiss psychologist Jean Piaget was one of the first to make sophisticated use of this metaphor (himself having been a child prodigy in the study of biology). But many others have built on and applied this metaphor in unique ways (e.g., Posner, Strike, Hewson, & Gertzog, 1982; Verula, Thompson, & Rosch, 1992). Often, researchers are interested in how the introduction of new *ideas* to the mind is like the introduction of new *species* to an ecosystem. Specifically, researchers investigate the interaction of new ideas with the preexisting concepts constituting the ecosystem of the mind. Let us explore this comparison.

When a new species is introduced into an existing ecosystem, three primary outcomes are possible. First, the new species may simply die off because it does not fit into the ecosystem. This is the most common outcome. Think of it this way: Of all the earth's fish species, how many could survive if introduced into Yellowstone Lake? The answer: very, *very* few. For the great majority of fish species, life would be very short because the environmental conditions and available resources simply do not match the needs of the species.

A second possible outcome is that the new species may become integrated into the ecosystem without causing major changes. This is rare in nature, but it is possible that a new species may fit into a new environmental niche and survive without causing major displacement of native species. For example, there may be a fish that does not eat the Yellowstone cutthroat or compete for the same food source, living space, and spawning areas. However, this is unlikely and if anyone proposes introducing a "compatible" fish to another lake with native cutthroat, let's just all agree it would be bad idea, ok?

The third possibility is the "invasive species takes over and wreaks havoc throughout the ecosystem" outcome, á la the lake trout in Yellowstone Lake. These outcomes parallel and shed light on learning outcomes. The following sections discuss these three outcomes in turn.

Why We Get the Cause of the Seasons Wrong

The first outcome, in which the introduced species simply dies because it does not fit the existing environment, is equivalent to non-learning. The new idea or knowledge simply does not fit with the individual's existing ideas, knowledge, and experiences. In fact, the new idea may be rejected because it conflicts with existing ideas.

In the early '80s, researchers discovered a perplexing phenomenon. Many science students entered the classroom with a set of ideas about how the world works and left the classroom with these same ideas intact, even after receiving instruction contradicting these beliefs. Remarkably, many of these existing beliefs persisted all the way through high school and college. Students showed a tenacious ability *not* to learn new ideas!

This phenomenon was illustrated cleverly in a video that has become a bit of cult classic among educators. The video, *A Private Universe*, was produced in 1987 by the Science Media Group at the Harvard-Smithsonian Center for Astrophysics. It opens with interviews conducted at a Harvard University graduation ceremony. Various graduates are shown responding to (seemingly) simple questions about the causes of the seasons and the phases of the moon. This content is something kids first learn in elementary school and study again in middle school and high school. Yet, these well-educated Harvard graduates respond by conveying some of the same incorrect beliefs commonly expressed by children.

Children often say summer is caused by the earth getting closer to the sun, and winter is caused by the earth getting farther away from the sun. In reality, the Earth's orbit is nearly circular, and distance has nothing to do with the cause of the seasons. Nothing at all. Yet, here is the response of an intelligent Harvard graduate who took a course in physics, relativity, and —yes—planetary motion: "OK. I think the seasons happen because as the earth travels around the sun, it gets nearer to the sun, which produces warmer weather, and gets farther away, which produces colder weather." *Are you kidding me?* How is such a thing possible?

It is possible and actually quite common (go ask your friends about the cause of the seasons) because, according to the constructivist perspective, the mind is an active conceptual ecosystem where ideas battle it out in a survival-of-the-fittest competition. New ideas often never make it because they cannot get a foothold in the ecology, and are outcompeted by existing ideas.

To illustrate, let's go back to the cause of the seasons. Again, many kids erroneously connect the seasons to the distance between the earth and sun. Why is this belief so common? Well, consider the child's existing conceptual ecology. Children have many experiences with heat sources such as fires and space heaters, leading to the conclusion that the closer you get to a heat source, the warmer it is. This idea becomes a central feature of the conceptual ecology. When considering the cause of the seasons, believing that the earth moves closer to and farther away from the sun makes complete logical sense given the existing conceptual ecology.

"Logical sense" is a key criterion of "fitness" in the conceptual ecology metaphor. Those ideas that most logically fit with existing ideas and most logically explain events in the world are the most fit. Simply put, the most fit ideas are the ones that make the most sense.

Now consider the scientifically correct (but still incomplete) idea kids are taught about the cause of the seasons: the seasons are caused by the earth rotating around the sun on a tilt so that sometimes the sun's rays hit a particular part of the earth directly (summer) and sometimes indirectly (winter). First of all, this is a much more complex explanation that often does not make much sense. Second, this whole idea of direct and indirect rays is very abstract and not immediately plausible.

Children may ask themselves, "The *angle* of the sun's rays is the difference between 100-degree weather and freezing weather? Really? Why would the angle make any difference at all?" Consequently, this new idea is often outcompeted by the existing idea that makes total sense. Sure, kids will parrot back what they know is *supposed* to be the correct answer, but when pushed or after time has passed, they revert to the original idea. By analogy, it is as if the introduced species hangs around on the periphery of the ecosystem for while but eventually dies off. This outcome is all too common.

Why It Took 1,500 Years to Change an Idea

The second outcome, in which the new species fits into and survives in the existing ecosystem without causing a major change to the ecosystem, is equivalent to the learning outcome that Piaget referred to as *assimilation*. Assimilation occurs when we fit new information or knowledge into our existing conceptual ecosystem without substantially altering that ecosystem.

Again, there is nearly always *some* change to the existing ecosystem when a new species is introduced, and the same is true of our conceptual ecosystems when new information is added. However, if this change is relatively minor or insignificant, we call it assimilation.

Now, you may be thinking to yourself, *Wait a minute. This assimilation thing sounds just like the* mind as Internet *metaphor. It's just new information being added to an existing network.* And if you were thinking this, you would be correct. As presented so far, assimilation is just like adding new links and web pages. But it is not always that simple. Things get a bit more complex and interesting when we look at the constructive side of assimilation. That is, when we look at how we often transform and alter new information to *make* it assimilate into our existing ideas and beliefs.

Watson and Konicek (1990) provided a great example of how we often transform information so that it can be assimilated into our existing beliefs. They described an elementary classroom where the kids believed warm clothes were warm because they produced heat. Following good constructivist pedagogy, the teacher decided to let the students test their theory. The students set up experiments all around the room. They grabbed thermometers, wrapped them in hats, gloves, and sweaters, and left them overnight to heat up. The next day, much to the kids' surprise, the thermometer readings remained unchanged.

Did the kids immediately conclude that their existing ideas were wrong and go about modifying their conceptual ecosystems? Of course not! Instead, they began to modify their ideas about the experiments so the results could be assimilated with prior beliefs. They concluded the experiments did not work because air got in or there was not enough time for the thermometers to change.

They tried the experiments again, using a longer duration and blocking airflow by using plastic bags, closets, and desk drawers. However, the kids were again disappointed when the thermometers still read room temperature. Surely now the kids would begin to question their theory of warm clothes producing heat, right? No. Instead, some concluded the thermometers were broken. Others simply said they did not know what was going on.

At this point, it would be easy to claim these kids were simply being stubborn. However, explaining their behavior solely in terms of stubbornness is similar to explaining reactions to the O.J. Simpson trial evidence solely in terms of racial bias. Doing so misses the key point: we interpret and make sense of new information in terms of our existing knowledge and beliefs. The kids were simply interpreting the data in ways that made sense given what they already knew. Invariably, this process of interpretation results in a transformation of the new information. This point is worth repeating. *New information is changed to fit with our existing ideas.*

We often preserve the fundamental ideas of our conceptual ecosystem by allowing more peripheral ideas to change. Watson and Konicek (1990) use the metaphor of core beliefs and protective belt beliefs. Core beliefs are those that occupy a more central position in the ecosystem. They provide a foundation for many other beliefs. Consequently, a change in a core belief necessitates changes in a whole host of other beliefs. Protective belt beliefs exist more on the periphery of the ecosystem and can be changed without causing massive restructuring. In fact, they are often changed to *preserve* the fundamental structure of the ecosystem.

A historical example illustrates this point. In ancient times, most people believed the earth was the center of the universe. They thought the sun, moon, stars, and planets revolved around our home planet. This belief held a central place in the collective conceptual ecology for a number of reasons.

First, it made sense given a whole lot of other experiential knowledge. For instance, it certainly *looks* like the sun, moon, and stars travel across the sky while the earth remains still. In addition, people reasoned that if the earth were moving we would feel the motion and be constantly subjugated to tremendous winds (of course, this conflict of ideas was probably never a problem for the ancient inhabitants of Chicago or Wyoming). Second, various religious perspectives viewed the earth as fixed in place. Third, the earth being the center of the universe fit with other beliefs about the importance and centrality of humans—*humph! It is not I that revolves but the universe that revolves around me!*

However, as far back as the ancient Greeks, observers of the heavens noted that celestial bodies did not always do what they were supposed to do; they did not conform to Plato's belief in uniform circular motion. For instance, it appeared that, over the course of a number of days, the planets moved east (relative to the stars), stopped, moved backward for a time, stopped again, and, finally, resumed moving eastward.

This backward progression, or retrograde motion, can easily be explained in models that have the earth and planets revolving around the sun. But most Greeks were not willing to give up their core belief in the earth being the center of the universe. Instead, they proposed that the planets revolved around in little circles, or epicycles, as they completed a larger revolution around the earth (see Figure 6.1).

This new model explained the retrograde motion while maintaining uniform circular motion and keeping the earth at the center of the universe where it belonged. But the theory still needed some tweaking by Ptolemy to fully match the observations. He added some points called deferents and equants and related the revolutions to these points. These tweaks made the circular motions slightly less uniform and moved the center of the revolutions to a spot just off the earth, but the model kept the earth fixed in place as the, more-or-less, center of the universe. As a result, the Ptolemic model endured for more than a *thousand* years.

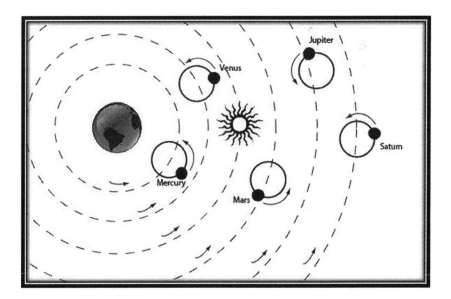

FIGURE 6.1.   Earth-Centered Model of the Universe With Planetary Epicycles.

Eventually, more problems arose with the idea of the earth being the center of the universe and, by 1543, Copernicus published a book arguing for a sun-centered universe. However, Tycho Brahe preserved the core belief in an earth-centered universe by proposing that the sun and moon revolved around a stationary earth, and the other five known planets revolved around the sun. Nevertheless, in December of 1610 (that's some 1,445 years after Ptolemy in case you're counting), Galileo provided solid evidence to back up Copernicus. He observed that Venus went through all phases just like the moon. Such an outcome made sense if Venus orbited the sun but not if Venus orbited the earth. This discovery, along with other work by Kepler, would eventually spell the doom of the earth-centered view of the universe (just don't tell the Flat Earth Society).

You have to admit the ancient astronomers were quite brilliant at designing ways to preserve their core beliefs. We exhibit similar levels of ingenuity when our core beliefs are challenged. We are very clever at transforming peripheral beliefs and assimilating new information in ways that preserve those ideas that are more central to our conceptual ecosystems. Of course, the result is that we are often remarkably intelligent about avoiding learning.

To summarize, assimilation occurs when new learning does not cause fundamental change to the existing conceptual ecosystem because it fits nicely and avoids conflicting with existing ideas/experiences/beliefs, is transformed to *make* it fit nicely, or causes peripheral changes to the conceptual ecosystem that allow core aspects to remain unchanged.

The Lake Trout in Yellowstone Lake

The third possible outcome when introducing a new species to an ecosystem is that it becomes an invasive species wreaking havoc throughout the ecosystem. This outcome is equivalent to what Piaget termed *accommodation* and other researchers have termed *conceptual change*. Invasive species are a disaster in nature, but an invasive species is exactly what we need for learning. When it comes to learning, we want the lake trout in Yellowstone Lake.

Accommodation or conceptual change can be defined as learning that results in fundamental changes to an individual's existing ideas and beliefs. Piaget and his colleagues developed a number of tasks that explore this kind of learning. Many of these "Piagetian tasks" involved a child or researcher manipulating a set of physical materials, allowing children to observe concrete outcomes that might conflict with initial beliefs.

When I teach my students about Piaget, I like to invite children into the classroom and have them engage in some of these Piagetian tasks. In one task, the children predict the movements of a balance. The balance consists of a beam resting on a pivot with five pegs on each side (see Figure 6.2). I place weights on different pegs and ask the children to predict what will happen.

Once I filmed my seven-year-old son, Hayden, doing this task. In the video, I place two weights on peg 1 on the left side. Then I place a weight on peg 5 on the

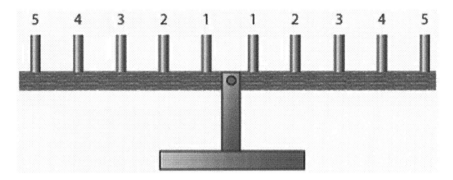

FIGURE 6.2.   Balance Used for the Piagetian Task.

right side while holding the balance steady. Next, I ask Hayden to predict what will happen. He predicts the balance will tip to the right. Kaya, his four-year old sister, then jumps in and exclaims that it will tip to the left. I let go of the balance, and it falls to the right (Kaya: "Hayden was riiiiight").

I move the weight on the right from the fifth peg to the third peg and again ask Hayden to predict what will happen. This time Hayden predicts it would balance. When I let go, it again tips to the right (Kaya: "Hayden was wrong!").

I next ask Hayden to move the weight onto the peg where he thinks it will balance. He moves it to the second peg and, when I let go, it balances. I then add two more weights to peg 1 on the left so there are a total of four weights on the peg (Kaya: "Oh, just like I'm four! Just like I'm four!"). I ask Hayden to move the weight on the right to the peg that will make it balance. Hayden sucks in his bottom lip, pauses, counts four pegs over, and then places the weight on the fourth peg. When I let go of the balance, it again stays level.

"How did you know it was going to balance?" I ask.

His eyes lighting up, Hayden responds, "Because last time there was two [touching peg one on the left] and on the second peg, we put it [touching the second peg on the right], and it balanced. And since there's four now, I put it on the fourth peg."

The above example illustrates a kid changing initial ideas and constructing new ones. This is accommodation. However, accommodation is not always this easy. For Hayden, the initial ideas were not deeply integrated and central to his conceptual ecology. He had some ideas about balances such as *if the weight is farther over on one side it will probably tip to that side*. But this was not a central idea upon which a number of other ideas depended. Consequently, when confronted with conflicting information, it was not too difficult to change the ideas and construct new ones.[1]

Accommodation is harder when it involves a richer and more expansive conceptual ecosystem with fundamental ideas that have a deep history and significance. Often, particular conditions are required for such accommodation to occur. Again, we can draw a parallel back to the lake trout in Yellowstone Lake.

As noted, most fish introduced into Yellowstone Lake would simply die, thus leaving the Yellowstone cutthroat and surrounding ecosystem unchanged. But the conditions were just right for the lake trout to become established and cause chaos. The lake trout evolved in cold, deep lakes just like Yellowstone Lake. Thus, it was adapted to survive in just this type of environment. Moreover, the Yellowstone cutthroat had evolved in a context free of other fish predators and had not developed defenses against such a predator. The conditions were just right; the results were inevitable.

The Nature of Scientific Revolutions

So what are the perfect conditions needed for accommodation? Posner et al. (1982) reasoned that we could learn a lot by studying the nature of scientific revolutions. For example, when the scientific community finally rejected the earth-centered view of the universe, what conditions were present? Why did the community finally make the change after some thousand years? Maybe those same general conditions need to be present for us to make fundamental changes to our own conceptual ecosystems.

Posner et al. settled on four conditions that they suggested were critical for both scientific revolutions and individual conceptual change. The first condition is the need for dissatisfaction with the existing theory. The scientific community is reluctant to give up an existing theory for some new fangled theory as long as the old one still works.

One of the reasons the earth-centered view of the universe persisted so long is simply that it worked. It explained the observations and predicted the motions of the planets. But as Galileo and others conducted new observations, the earth-centered models had to become more and more cumbersome. Eventually, the scientific community became dissatisfied with these models and open to the Copernican model.

Likewise, we often need to experience dissatisfaction with our existing beliefs before we are open to changing them. Our Harvard graduate likely clung to his belief linking the seasons to the distance between the earth and sun because he never really saw a problem with this explanation. He was probably told the correct explanation and never contemplated a question such as "How can it be summer in North America at the same time it is winter in South America?"

---

[1] But even though these ideas were not core ideas, they cannot be considered protective belt ideas. That is, they were not ideas that were changed in order to preserve some more deeply held idea.

We often associate learning with such positive mental states as clarity, understanding, peace, and harmony. However, there is actually a critical moment when such mental states as confusion, dissonance—or to use Piaget's term—*perturbation* are needed. We need that moment where we say to ourselves, "Wait a second. How *can* it be winter in South America in the middle of July? Something is wrong here." When my kids complain about how confusing their homework is, I like to respond, "Great! That means you are experiencing perturbation and are open to conceptual change!" Then my kids wander off and complain about how nonuseful it is to have a dad who's an educational psychologist.

According to Posner et al., the second and third conditions critical to scientific revolutions and individual conceptual change are that the new idea must be intelligible and plausible. That is, the idea has to make sense and be believable. For example, Einstein's theory of relativity did not cause an immediate revolution because many individuals could not make sense of it, and some of the claims seemed totally implausible. In fact, an early version of his Ph.D. dissertation containing the theory of relativity was rejected, seemingly because the professors found it too uncanny (Rigden, 2005).

What was so uncanny about the theory of relativity? Well, imagine some time in the future you board a spacecraft and go flying about the universe for a few years, traveling near the speed of light. When you return home, you find your kids are now older than you are! This bizarre and seemingly unbelievable scenario is actually predicted by one of the fundamental claims of Einstein's theory: time is relative. Only after developing some understanding of Einstein's theory and running experiments confirming some of his predictions did the scientific community collectively agree that maybe Einstein wasn't so crazy after all.[2]

Similarly, for us to accept a new idea that fundamentally changes our existing conceptual ecosystems, this new idea has to make sense and appear plausible. This may have been another factor working against our Harvard graduate. As mentioned previously, kids are often taught that the seasons are caused by direct and indirect light, but this explanation can be confusing and it does not seem very plausible.

The fourth condition identified by Posner et al. was that the new idea had to be fruitful in the sense that it opened up new areas of research and discovery. As applied to the individual, the condition of "fruitfulness" means that, for a new idea to have a chance at integrating into the existing conceptual ecosystem, it needs to prove fruitful in leading to personal insights and discoveries. Simply put, the idea should be meaningful and useful. Or, to jump ahead a few metaphors, it should be a map that guides students in having their own journey with the content (see chapter 9).

---

[2] Interestingly, in his later years, Einstein himself resisted the development of quantum mechanics theory for many of the same reasons. The theory did not make sense in terms of his conception of how the universe should be.

Wreaking Havoc

Given the necessity of these four conditions (dissatisfaction with the existing idea, intelligibility, plausibility, and fruitfulness of the new idea) it is understandable why accommodation is so hard. But sometimes it does happen. Sometimes deficiencies with existing ideas are acknowledged. Sometimes the new idea does make sense and is plausible. Sometimes it is meaningful and useful.

When this happens, when the conditions are just right, it is like the lake trout in Yellowstone Lake. The idea moves in and transforms the conceptual ecosystem; deep-level accommodation occurs. And when genuine, deep-level changes to the conceptual ecosystem occur, the consequences are far reaching. Just as the lake trout affected everything from pelicans to grizzly bears, so the new idea can affect many others. This point is well illustrated by another example of a scientific revolution.

When Sir Isaac Newton proposed his three laws of motion, he likely had little idea just how disruptive they would be. Prior to Newton, most people believed that some force or divine intervention was needed to keep the heavenly objects in motions. For instance, angels were believed to push the planets across the sky. Newton showed that such movement could be explained in terms of simple scientific principles and mathematical equations. This achievement obviously had a profound effect on physics, but that is not all.

Religious scholars began to rethink the nature of God. *If God is not needed to keep the universe running, maybe He is not as involved as we thought. Maybe He created the universe and set it in motion like a giant clockwork, and then stepped back to let it run on its own. Maybe God is not directly involved in our own lives either. Maybe He created us and left us to run on our own, too.*

In addition, Newton's equations proposed that if you knew the initial position and velocity of an object and could describe all the forces acting on it, then you could determine any future position and velocity of the object. Theoretically then, if you could determine the position, velocity, and acting forces for all the particles in someone's body, you could predict where they would be in the future. The logical conclusion then is that life must be pre-determined because we can predict where it will be in the future. Whether or not we do know the position, velocity, and acting forces for every particle in a body is irrelevant. Simply the fact that, theoretically, we *could* make such predictions means life must be pre-determined. Thus, determinism in philosophy was another effect of Newton's laws—yes, determinism goes way back beyond Skinner. And still, there is more.

Newton's laws offered an unprecedented potential to explain and predict the world. The world was no longer unknowable and incomprehensible. We could explain it without metaphysics. By explaining it, we could control it. This became the new worldview, the scientific worldview. And since that day, the world has never been the same. Our collective conceptual ecosystem was forever changed.

In the same way, new ideas can cause ripple effects that spread far and wide across our personal conceptual ecosystems. They disrupt prior ideas and may even shatter beliefs that once were core. In the chaos, new relationships between ideas are formed, and fragments of knowledge are pieced together into new understandings. Piaget believed that this process of disruption and reconstruction was at the heart of learning. Not only was it necessary to develop more sophisticated ideas (or *schemas*), but it was the key process by which we developed more advanced levels of thought.

The Assimilation and Accommodation Dance

Nearly all learning involves both assimilation and accommodation to a certain degree. That is, there is nearly always some assimilation of new ideas into the existing conceptual ecosystem and some change to the ecosystem itself. Indeed, many learning episodes may best be described as a balanced interplay or "dance" between the two. The following example illustrates the processes of assimilation and accommodation occurring together, and how a conceptual ecosystem functions as an evolving set of interconnected ideas.

In the aforementioned video of my kids' ideas about the world, I asked my eleven-year-old daughter, Sierra, to explain the cause of the seasons. She said,

"Because the earth goes around the sun and it's facing the same way. [Sierra makes a fist with her right hand to represent the sun and holds up her left hand to represent the earth with her palm facing her fist] so right now this would get direct sunlight [nods toward her palm.] [Sierra then moves her hand around her fist without rotating it so that the back of her hand now faces her fist] but then it doesn't get exactly direct sunlight."

"What do you mean by direct sunlight?" I ask.

"Where there's like…[she holds her fist and hand up again with the palm facing her fist.] [Pointing at the back of her hand] this isn't getting direct sunlight because the sun's here [makes a fist again and puts it in front of her palm.] Like whatever side's facing it is the side that gets the direct sunlight and then whatever side is not facing it, it isn't getting direct sunlight."

Sierra has constructed her own unique understanding of direct and indirect light. Like many kids, she used her existing conceptual ecosystem to come to a logical conclusion about the meaning of direct and indirect light. She has faced the sun and felt the heat on her face and turned away and felt it cool. She has experience using the term *direct* in reference to some object moving straight to another object without any interference or deviation in course, such as "Dad, can't we go directly back to camp? Do we have to fish every stream and lake?" (*Yes, yes we do Sierra*). Given these experiences, her conception of direct and indirect light makes total sense.

In the video, I decide to cause a bit of dissonance and see what happens. I begin to ask her about the difference between the cause of the seasons and the cause of day and night. I am thinking she will immediately say, "Oh yeah. I was getting those mixed up." But I am wrong. Sierra doesn't see any conflict at all. Therefore, to fig-ure out what's going on with her conceptual ecosystem, I grab a light to represent the sun and an orange to represent the earth. Then I shine the light on the orange and say, "So here's day. [I spin the orange 180 degrees] here's night. But you were saying the same thing is the seasons."

Sierra grabs the orange out of my hand, moves it in a circle around the light and explains, "When it's going around it's not staying there as long because it is going around much slower. Because this is a day [spins the orange] and this is a year [moves the orange around the light.] So it's staying in one place a lot longer."

There is more to her theory than I initially thought. It is not just that she is confusing the cause of the seasons with the cause of day and night. She has appar-ently reasoned out that if the earth rotated around the sun without spinning, then some of the year, part of the earth would be directly facing the sun and some of the year it will not. She knows the earth does spin but has not fully reconciled the meaning of this with her other idea. Well, I could not resist trying to cause more dissonance. So I took the orange, shined the light on it and asked, "Is this day or is this summer?"

After a brief hesitation, Sierra responds, "That's day. [Then she looks at me out of the corner of her eyes and scrunches her nose as if to say, "What are you up to Dad?"]

"Show me, what's the difference between day in the summer and day in the winter?" I ask.

"Well cuz…" Sierra looks up, purses her lips at me, then laughs and bites her lip.

"Now you're stumped, huh?"

"No." There's a long pause. Then Sierra, with a half a smile, says, "You're an-noying that way. You always ask annoying questions and then try to make them so complex they last ten minutes long."

She's on to me! What's interesting about this response is that Sierra is still fairly convinced that her explanation is correct. She thinks I am just failing to un-derstand and trying to confuse her (she was well on her way to being a teenager). However, there must be some degree of dissatisfaction slowly developing because Sierra starts playing around with an additional explanation.

She takes the orange in her left hand and holds it in front of the light. Then she places her right index finger horizontally across the center of the orange, indicat-ing that her finger represents the equator. Next, she explains, "The sun isn't going like this [she uses her finger to draw a curving arc that goes up from the light to the top of the orange.] It is just going like this [she draws a straight line with her finger from the light to the center of the orange]. It hits where the equator is sticking out the most [she uses her finger to represent the equator again and wiggles it away from the orange.] Like things along the equator stick out the most."

A couple things may be going on here. It appears the idea of indirect light is starting to evolve. My guess is that Sierra is recalling prior science lessons in which the teacher said something about direct rays hitting the equator and indirect rays hitting the edges of the earth. It is as if this knowledge was lying dormant in the conceptual ecology, like a frog that was hibernating but now is emerging from the mud to become involved in the ecosystem. The classic idea of distance causing the seasons also seems to be reemerging. This is the grizzly bear emerging from its den. But now, instead of the whole earth getting closer to the sun, the theory is that some parts of the earth stick out and thus are warmer because they are closer.

I certainly assume this is what she is thinking and ask, "The equator sticks out the most so that is the hottest?"

"Yeah," Sierra responds confidently.

"So it gets cooler on the top and the bottom because they are farther away?"

"Yeah. So that is why Hawaii [pointing at the middle of the orange] is hotter than Canada [pointing at the upper part of the orange]."

So now we have an evolved conceptual ecosystem where indirect rays curve before hitting the earth and direct rays go straight to the earth. Places like the equator are hotter because they receive these direct rays and they are closer to the sun. But this still does not explain why we have the different seasons. The idea about parts of the earth spending more time facing the sun at certain times of the year seems to be on hold for the moment. So I ask my money question, "How does it get so it is summer up here [pointing to the upper hemisphere of the orange] and winter down here [pointing to the lower hemisphere?]"

I am sure Sierra is going to respond with the classic mutated form of the distance explanation, which is this: the earth is tilted on its axis so as it rotates around the sun, sometimes the northern hemisphere is tilted toward the sun and is closer, hence summer. Sometimes it is tilted away and is more distant, hence winter. I can picture Sierra's conceptual ecosystem about to evolve in this way. I am excited to watch it happen even though I know I am fostering another misconception. But Sierra has had enough of this nonsense. She grabs the orange and says, "Maybe it spins this way" as she laughs and makes the orange spin vertically while corkscrewing it around the light.

Is this example assimilation or accommodation? It is both. Sierra is using her existing beliefs, ideas, and experiences to make sense of the world, and new information is transformed and assimilated into this conceptual ecosystem (i.e., direct light interpreted as light directly hitting the earth). But even though this information has been transformed or interpreted through the lens of her existing beliefs, it still carries a bit of dissonance (i.e., does direct light equal summer or does it equal day?). This dissonance causes some accommodation of the ecosystem. Dormant ideas are awakened and new connections are made (i.e., maybe it does has something to do with distance; but instead of the whole earth getting closer to the sun, parts stick out).

The change is not an immediate and radical restructuring—it is not the lake trout in Yellowstone Lake—but it is a change. A small evolution of the conceptual ecosystem has taken place. Over time, as more information is encountered, it will continue to evolve, often in unpredictable ways.

Such is learning from a constructivist perspective. It is not a matter of adding another brick to the wall or node to the network. It is a matter of how we interpret new ideas and make sense of them in terms of existing ideas. It is a matter of how existing ideas are transformed and restructured in light of the new ideas. It is a matter of a living, evolving conceptual ecosystem.

Where the Metaphor Breaks Down

The conceptual ecosystem metaphor suggests that the mind is comprised of competing ideas. Those ideas that best help us explain and make sense of the world in a consistent way, are the most "fit" ideas and most likely to become integral parts of our conceptual ecologies. But are we really so rational?

Consider the following example adapted from a case study recorded by Demastes, Good, and Peebles (1995). Tyler is a senior in high school taking Biology II. She comes from a religious background and, more or less, believes in the Biblical account of the creation in a literal way. That is, she generally believes that God created Adam and Eve and all the creatures of the earth a relatively short time ago. In her biology class, she encounters scientific theories about evolution and the age of the earth. She must have encountered these theories before, but apparently never dealt with them in a serious way. This time it is different.

As the instruction progresses, Tyler comes to modify her belief about the creation and age of the earth. She accepts that the earth is much older than she previously thought and adopts a belief that God created the earth's creatures over a long period by guiding the evolutionary process. Now here is the interesting part. Tyler's belief change has very little to do with the theories providing a more sensible account of the scientific data. It is not even clear whether she finds the theories intelligible, plausible, and fruitful. So why would Tyler change a core belief?

The answer is dinosaurs. Dinosaurs are cool. Tyler likes dinosaurs. Prior to the instruction, she had not realized there was a conflict between believing in dinosaurs and believing in the recent creation of the earth. Therefore, when the conflict arose, she accepted the idea of an older earth and evolution so she could keep believing in dinosaurs. As Demastes et al. (1995) put it, "For Tyler the world was old not because of an array of supporting evidence, but because it had to be old in order for dinosaurs to have existed" (p. 660). Tyler is not changing her beliefs based strictly on the degree to which competing ideas best explain the world. Her belief change is motivated primarily by her affection for dinosaurs.

Many educational theorists now believe that emotions and motivation play a central role in either facilitating or inhibiting change in our ideas. Think about the political conversations you have had with friends. Can we explain political beliefs purely in terms of rational logic? Not likely. We can still think about the mind as an ecosystem, but we need to think about it as a conceptual *and emotional* ecosystem. Or, if you prefer, an ecosystem comprised of emotional concepts.

Emotions play a particularly important role in determining our core beliefs. Previously, I implied that our core beliefs are our fundamental ways of making sense of the world. This is true, but it is an oversimplification. Broad explanatory power is but one characteristic of core beliefs. A second characteristic is emotional attachment. For many of us, our most core beliefs are those that could be described as religious and cultural beliefs. To a large degree, it is because these beliefs connect to our identity—our sense of "this is who I am" and "this is the group of people I belong to." Identity is more emotional than rational. It is a felt purpose, a felt connection.

If we reflect back to the O.J. Simpson trial, does this mean that the judgments of innocence or guilt made by different groups really were just reflections of bias after all? No, not at all. But we do need to recognize that both experience and identity played vital roles in the development of the respective worldviews about policemen. We also need to recognize that these worldviews are comprised of emotional concepts. Perhaps the judgments can best be explained as individuals making sense of the evidence through their worldviews while recognizing that such individuals are motivated to preserve their worldviews, and these worldviews cannot be separated from one's sense of identity.

IMPLICATIONS

Given the richness of the mind as ecosystem metaphor, there are numerous implications to be considered. These are discussed below with a few extra metaphors thrown in.

Prior Knowledge Is a Double-Edged Sword

In the Information Processing perspective, prior knowledge is seen as almost universally beneficial. Prior knowledge in the form of ideas, facts, and experiences constituted the network to which new information can be attached and secured. But in the conceptual ecosystem metaphor, the relationship between prior knowledge and learning is more complex. Prior knowledge both fosters and hinders learning.

It fosters learning in the sense that no learning is possible without prior knowledge. Just as no organism can survive apart from an ecosystem, so no knowledge can exist apart from an existing conceptual ecosystem. However, this conceptual ecosystem may resist the introduction of new ideas that threaten its stability. Thus, new ideas are often rejected or transformed as a consequence of prior knowledge.

We Need Time to Work With Our Ideas

This implication flows from the first one. Because we have prior ideas that are deeply embedded in a conceptual ecosystem, they are not easy to give up and they do not just go away. If we truly want to change an existing conceptual ecology then we need to work with these ideas in a meaningful way. Specifically, we need an opportunity to test them and discover their limits. For individuals to overcome a belief that the seasons are caused by distance from the sun, they need to explore the circumstances in enough depth to understand why a distance explanation is problematic. Simply telling someone the seasons are not caused by distance from the sun is generally ineffective over the long term.

We also need time to work with new ideas in order for these ideas to survive and take root in the conceptual ecosystem. Individuals need time to make sense of an idea like direct and indirect light, explore how this idea could explain different phenomena, and maybe do their own experiments or investigations. Unfortunately, when individuals learn new concepts in a typical school way, which is to memorize terms and definitions, they keep these ideas on the periphery of the conceptual ecosystem, where they soon die off.

Don't Bend the Map

In the book *Deep Survival: Who Lives, Who Dies, and Why*, Laurence Gonzales (2003) writes about what happens when individuals get lost in the wilderness. He describes being lost as the psychological phenomenon of your mental map not matching up with your physical surroundings. You have a mental image of where such things as the trail, the lake, the valley, or the campsite *should be*. But they aren't there. This disconnect is terribly distressing.

To reduce the anxiety, we try to make the physical world fit our mental map by tweaking reality. Edward Cornell, a psychologist quoted by Gonzalez puts it this way, "Whenever you start looking at your map and saying something like, 'Well, that lake could have dried up,' or 'That boulder could have moved,' a red light should go off. You're trying to make reality conform to your expectations rather than seeing what's there. In the sport of orienteering, they call that 'bending the map'" (pp. 163–164).

Bending the map is exactly what we do when we try to assimilate conflicting new ideas into our existing conceptual ecosystem. Bending the map is what ancient astronomers did when they created epicycles, deferents, and equants to keep the earth at the center of the universe. Bending the map is what the elementary kids did when they maintained their belief about warm clothes producing heat by concluding that air got it, there was not enough time, and the thermometer was broken.

Lord, Ross, and Lepper (1979) provided a remarkable illustration of this point in a study of attitudes about capital punishment. They recruited 24 individuals in favor of capital punishment and 24 individuals against it to participate in the study. The participants were given two fictional research studies to read. One study provided evidence supporting the argument that capital punishment deters murder. The other study provided evidence undermining this argument. You might think that studying evidence on both sides of the issue would make the participants more moderate in their opinions or at least more understanding of the other viewpoint. You might think this, but you would be wrong.

The participants actually became *more polarized* than they were before the study! Why? Because they bent the map. They discredited the evidence that conflicted with their initial belief by focusing on flaws in the research. Simultaneously, they ignored the *same* flaws in research that supported their initial belief. They bent reality to make it fit their expectations and desires.

In *Deep Survival*, Gonzalez (2003) explains how the survivors, those who get lost and are able to find their way back again, are those who realize they have to reconstruct their mental map. They admit that reality does not match their existing map, and they start to create a fresh one based on what they can see. But, as anyone who has become lost in the wilderness can attest, this is very hard to do. It is hard to admit that you are truly lost, that your mental map is truly out of sync with reality. Likewise, it is so much easier to modify new ideas so they fit our existing beliefs. It is so much easier to discredit or ignore conflicting information.

But if you want to advance your conceptual ecosystem, this is exactly what you have to avoid. You have to face reality. Even if it is painful, uncomfortable, and confusing, you have to acknowledge the disconnect and begin reconstructing your conceptual ecosystem. You can never remove all your biases and preconceived notions, but you can ask yourself, "Am I bending the map? Am I seeing reality or am I seeing what I want to see? Am I understanding this as it really is or am I trying to force my own naïve understanding on it?" Asking these questions may just save you from remaining lost in the wilderness of misunderstanding.

Being Lost (and Found) Is a Good Thing

Piaget (1964) was primarily interested in figuring out how we get smart. How do we learn to think abstractly? How do we learn to think critically? This process of developing more advanced ways of thinking is called cognitive development, and Piaget (1970) identified various stages of cognitive development. Further, Piaget (1964) proposed that the process of equilibration is key to cognitive development and advancing from one stage to the next. Equilibration basically involves getting lost and finding your way back again.

On most occasions, our existing ideas for making sense of the world match up with the information we are processing about the world. Our mental map matches reality (at least as we perceive it). But then things happen to disrupt the harmony between our ideas and the world. We may encounter conflicting information or discover a logical flaw. Suddenly, there is a disturbing disconnect between our mental map and reality. We are lost.

Now we have a choice. We can either bend the map or we can reconstruct our personal mental map. If we choose the latter and reconstruct our conceptual ecosystem to account for the new information or new idea, then we have chosen the path of cognitive development. We have restored an equilibrium with the environment by reconstructing our existing beliefs. Piaget (1964) proposed that by engaging in this process over and over, we advance cognitively. We learn to think.

Ideas as Invasive Species

Some organisms have a unique potential to survive and thrive in new environments. These are the animals and plants that we disdainfully refer to as invasive species. Creatures like the zebra mussel, the brown rat, or—get this—the European rabbit. Yes, the cute, innocent looking rabbit is one of the most destructive species on earth. It has been introduced in countries across the globe and has had a massive impact on local environments. The greatest impact has been in Australia.

Legend has it that in 1859, Thomas Austin released 24 European rabbits into the wild in Australia. Austin was an avid hunter from England and wanted to bring the sport of rabbit hunting with him to Australia. Apparently, Austin was a bad shot, because these 24 rabbits soon created a rabbit epidemic that spread across the country. These rabbits caused chaos in the ecosystems by destroying local vegetation, causing soil erosion, and becoming food for other non-native species such as foxes and feral cats. In fact, rabbits are the prime culprits in the extinction of nearly an eighth of the mammals in Australia!

Now, carry this analogy over to ideas. Are some ideas like the rabbit? Do they have a unique potential to take root in our conceptual ecologies and cause massive change? One of my professors in graduate school, Dick Prawat, liked to talk about ideas in this way. He argued that, as educators, we often underestimated the potential of powerful ideas. His point was that we focus a lot on *how* to teach content: what strategies to use, how to accommodate individual differences, and so on. But we neglect to deeply consider *what* content we teach. That is, we do not spend equivalent effort contemplating what the most powerful ideas are within a particular topic.

Dr. Prawat compared ideas to critters and argued that some of these critters "have legs" and can run off in a number of directions. He liked to quote the great American educator John Dewey (1933/1986) who wrote, "There is no mistake more common in schools than ignoring the self-propelling power of an idea. Once it is aroused, an alert mind fairly races along with it. Of itself it carries the student into new fields; it branches out into new ideas as a plant sends forth new shoots" (p. 335).

Are some ideas like this? Do some ideas have much greater potential for transforming our conceptual ecosystems than others? Dr. Prawat shared with me the story of how he got his teenage son hooked on a powerful idea. He was watching a TV show about Gandhi when his son walked by. He tried to get his son to sit down and watch with him, but his son, being the teenager that he was, was not so inclined. As his son was walking away, Dr. Prawat called out, "This man brought Churchill to his knees." His son stopped and looked at the skinny man in sparse Indian garb displayed on the screen. Then Dr. Prawat sprung the big idea: *moral authority is more powerful than military authority.*

His son was hooked, and this idea became an invasive species. Many discussions followed about situations where moral authority trumped military authority or other sources of physical might. Such discussions expanded to considerations of foreign strategy (e.g., Can a country succeed militarily only to lose power by losing moral authority?) and such issues as what moral authority means in terms of personal relationships and whether it is really more influential than other forms of power such as wealth and status. The idea had legs.

But why? What is it about this idea that makes it so powerful? What is it about other ideas that makes them compelling? Unfortunately, the research community does not have good answers to these questions. Perhaps that will change in the future. On the other hand, perhaps these are questions that cannot really be answered by science. In either case, it is worth keeping in mind that some ideas may be more invasive than others.

REFERENCES

Demastes, S. S., Good, R. G., & Peebles, P. (1995). Students' conceptual ecologies and the process of conceptual change in evolution. *Science Education, 79,* 637–666. doi:10.1002/sce.3730790605

Dewey, J. (1933/1986). How we think: A restatement of the relation of reflective thinking to the educative process. In J. A. Boydston (Ed.), *John Dewey: The later works. 1925–1953* (Vol. 8, pp. 105–352). Carbondale, IL: Southern Illinois University Press. (Original work published 1933)

Gonzalez, L. (2003). *Deep survival: Who lives, who dies, and why.* New York, NY: Norton.

Gresswell, R. E. (2009, June 30). *Yellowstone cutthroat trout (Oncorhynchus clarkii bouvieri): A technical conservation assessment.* USDA Forest Service, Rocky Mountain Region. Retrieved August 18, 2010, from http://www.fs.fed.us/r2/projects/scp/assessments/yellowstonecutthroattrout.pdf.

Licis, K. (2010, April 18). Cutthroat enemy: Dreaded lake trout. *The Denver Post.* Retrieved from http://www.denverpost.com/extremes/ci_14905995.

Lord, C. G., Ross, L., & Lepper, M. R. (1997). Biased assimilation and attitude polarization: The effects of prior theories on subsequently considered evidence. *Journal of Personality and Social Psychology, 37,* 2098–2109. doi:10.1037/0022-3514.37.11.2098

Piaget, J. (1964). Development and learning. In R. E. Ripple & V. N. Rockcastle (Eds.), *Piaget rediscovered. A report of the Conference on Cognitive Studies and Curriculum Development* (pp. 38–46). Ithaca, NY: Cornell University.

Piaget, J. (1970). Piaget's theory. In P. Mussen (Ed.), *Charmichael's manual of child psychology* (3rd ed., pp. 703–732). New York: Wiley.

Posner, G. J., Strike, K. A., Hewson, P. W., & Gertzog, W. A. (1982). Accommodation of a scientific conception: Toward a theory of conceptual change. *Science Education, 66,* 211–227. doi:10.1002/sce.3730660207

Rigden, J. S. (2005). *Einstein 1905: The standard for greatness.* Cambridge, MA: Harvard University Press.

Ruzycki, J. R., Beauchamp, D. A., & Yule, D. L. (2003). Effects of introduced lake trout on native cutthroat trout in Yellowstone Lake. *Ecological Applications, 13,* 23–37. doi:10.1890/1051-0761(2003)013[0023:EOILTO]2.0.CO;2

Tanner, T. (2013). Fly fishing: Biologists at Yellowstone National Park and conservationists have embarked on an aggressive plan to bring back cutthroat trout. *Sporting Classics, Jan/Feb,* 65–68.

Verula, F., Thompson, E., & Rosch, E. (1992). *The embodied mind: Cognitive science and human experience.* Cambridge, MA: MIT Press.

Watson, B., & Konicek, R. (1990). Teaching for conceptual change: Confronting children's experience. *Phi Delta Kappan, May,* 680–686.

PART 4

SOCIOCULTURALISM

The cognitive and constructivist perspectives provided great insight about the individual mind. However, human beings are social creatures, and the individual mind does not function independently from society and culture. Thus, to fully understand learning, we need to add social and cultural perspectives to our repertoire of learning theories.

In a sense, behaviorism is a social perspective because it addresses how society shapes behavior. However, in this theory, society and culture are reduced to reinforcers and punishers. The theory does not address the complexities of society and culture and how these contribute to the development of the mind. Fortunately, theories have emerged that place particular emphasis on the role of society and culture in learning. These theories are the focus of Part Four.

In chapters 7 and 8, I discuss two metaphors central to the sociocultural perspective: *the mind as cultural tools* and *knowledge as cockroach or panda bear*. As you may have guessed, the first metaphor was conceived by a seminal figure in educational psychology, and second by…um…me.

CHAPTER 7

MIND AS CULTURAL TOOLS

In the early1900s, Lev Vygotsky was a Russian psychologist interested in study-ing cognitive development, particularly the development of consciousness. This was not a good position to be in. Directly studying cognition was politically incor-rect in Stalin's Russia and being politically incorrect resulted in your head getting chopped off. Stalin emphasized a Marxist tradition focusing on labor and social forms (i.e., practices, societal structures) resulting from different types of labor. Cognition was considered an abstract idea that did not exist in the real material world and the study of it reeked of idealism1.

However, Vygotsky found a clever way to study cognition. He used human and societal evolution as metaphors for cognitive development, thus linking the development of social forms to cognition and being a good Marxist (sort of: his works were banned, but that is a story for another day) (Prawat, 2000). More precisely, Vygotsky reasoned that the processes critical to the development of the human species and human societies would also be critical to the development of individual cognition (Vygotsky, 1978, 1986). Turns out, his reasoning was spot

---

[1] It is a bit more complex than this, obviously. The main point is that, for Stalin, Marxist dialectical and historical materialism was "good" and idealism was "bad." Studying cognition directly put you in danger of being on the idealism side.

Computers, Cockroaches, and Ecosystems: Understanding Learning through Metaphor,
pages 109–126.
109

on, but it begs the question, what are the processes critical to both human and societal evolution?

The human evolution question can be addressed by considering what makes humans unique from other animals. You can probably figure this out for yourself, but I am going to illustrate it through a fishing story because, quite frankly, I enjoy telling fishing stories—and this one includes a bear.

The Brooks River in Alaska is famous for its fishing, and even more famous for its bears. Dozens of brown bears converge on the river each season to do their own fishing. Because of all the bears, there are strict rules for the human fishermen. First, you have to stay at least 50 yards from the bears. Second, if you have a fish on your line and a bear approaches, you must break the fish off because you do not want (a) the fish splashing around and attracting the bear and (b) the bears to start associating fishermen with an easy meal. Third, and above all, fish caught must be immediately returned to the water because you do not want to get caught holding a fish when a bear comes by.

Well, one day I am fishing and the river is bursting at the seams. Sockeye salmon by the hundreds are running through the river and bears are chasing them all over the place. I am just trying to avoid the bears and catch the big rainbow trout hiding by the banks and avoiding the stampede of salmon. Well, I happen to hook the fish of the trip: a huge rainbow trout that sends me chasing after it down river. Luckily, there are no bears in my path, and after a long battle, I land the fish on a shallow gravel bar. Elated, I scoop up the fish. As I am holding this trophy fish, I hear a noise behind me. I glance over my shoulder and there, not ten feet away from me, emerging through the shoulder-high grass, is the head of an Alaskan brown bear.

So here I am, breaking all the bear rules and fearing that I am about to be the turf in a bear's surf and turf meal. What is worse, I cannot just drop the fish in the water because the water is only two or three inches deep for 15 feet in all directions. If I drop the fish, it is going to splash and make a huge commotion at my feet. So I hug the fish against my chest, where I hope it is out of sight, and waddle sideways upstream with my back to the bear, clinging desperately to the wiggling fish, until the water is deep enough for me to throw it in. Once the fish is released, I look back to check on the bear.

Now this is the important part and the point of the whole story. When I look back the bear is still staring at me, with a look on its face that says, "You are pathetic." Then, as if to prove its superiority, the bear leaps in the river, pounces on a salmon, and turns back to look at me with the salmon wiggling in its jaws.

It is hard not to realize the depths of your pitiful nature at a moment like this. To even be out here, I need a pair of waders, long underwear, fleece pants, a fleece jacket, a rain jacket, a wool hat, and fingerless gloves. To catch a fish, I have a fly rod and reel plus a fishing vest stuffed with half a fly shop. The bear needs none of this. The bear is a brute force of nature. And this is the difference between humans and other animals. In a word, we are pathetic without our tools.

But with our tools…oh my. We rule with our tools. We can make tools to help us survive and thrive in virtually any environment. We are not so great at catching salmon with our jaws like a bear, but we can construct elaborate fishing equipment to help us out. In fact, we only use fishing equipment to make it sporting. We could use a gill net and become much more efficient than the bears. Further, if we had to fight the bears for those salmon, our pathetic nature could be offset by the presence of a gun. Humans rule because we construct way better tools.

There is another important difference between animals and humans: language. We have it, they do not. To be fair to the animals, they can communicate. Birds can sing songs that carry meaning, bees can do a dance to convey distance and direction, orcas have unique family vocalizations, and so on. Yukon hunting guides have been known to interpret the calls of wolves, so we know they have a basic language. But even they cannot hold a candle to us. Our language is infinitely more advanced.

The acquisition of tools and the development of language: these are the two processes most often discussed as the keys to the development of humans as a species. And we get much the same picture when we look at the critical processes involved in the development of human society. Think about it. How do anthropologists and historians talk about our history? They talk about it in terms of the tools, right? The Stone Age. The Bronze Age. The Industrial Age. The Information Age. All these ages are defined by the dominant tools. By developing more advanced tools, societies grow and prosper.

Language is another key process that we use to talk about our history and describe societies. In fact, we often categorize societies as oral or written societies because modes of language use are so fundamental to the nature of the society. Socrates, by the way, thought written language was a terrible idea. He thought books would greatly hinder learning because you cannot argue, debate, and have interactive dialogue with a book. Plus, books would become a crutch for memory (Langham, 1994). In some ways, he was right. But he failed to realize the degree to which books would advance society by facilitating the creation and dispersal of knowledge. He failed to comprehend the power of this particular tool.

The importance of tools and language to human and societal evolution should be clear. But how did Vygotsky use these as metaphors for theorizing about the evolution of an individual's thinking?

MAKING SENSE OF THE METAPHOR

Three-Second Math

Try the following task: add the five 3-digit numbers listed below without using any external aid. Just, do the math in your head.

497
348
245
823
767

Could you do it? If so, how long did it take? If you are like me, it probably took you a while. Actually, if you are like me, you probably forgot the first part of the answer halfway through, added individual digits wrong, and started reaching for a pencil (the correct answer, by the way, is 2,680).

James Stigler (1984) discovered that certain eleven-year-old Chinese students could solve this problem in just three seconds. Three seconds! What is more, there was nothing remarkable about these students. They did not have genius level IQs. They were not mathematical savants. The only thing unique about them was that they had been trained in the use of the abacus.

The abacus is sort of like the original calculator. It consists of a set of bars with moveable beads (see Figure 7.1). By moving the beads around, you can perform various mathematical calculations. Many students in China are taught to use the abacus as part of their math instruction. In Taiwan, at the time of Stigler's study, students were introduced to the abacus in fourth grade and could become abacus experts through an optional after-school program.

Stigler studied the students in the after-school program and discovered that they were able to complete lengthy math problems extremely quickly and almost effortlessly using the abacus. This is not a shock given that the abacus is a highly

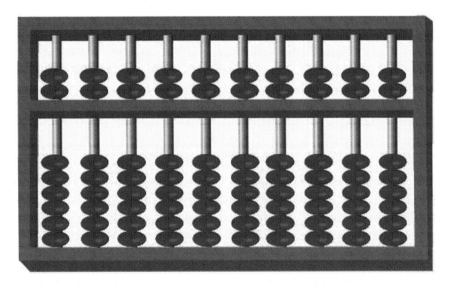

FIGURE 7.1. The abacus. (Figure created by Sierra Pugh.)

efficient aid for performing certain mathematical calculations. Stigler's noteworthy observation was that the students advanced to a point where they did not actually need the abacus to use the abacus. They could just *picture* the abacus in their minds and picture themselves moving the beads in the appropriate manner to solve a problem, such as adding five 3-digit numbers. And solve it they did. In a remarkable three seconds. The abacus allowed these students to become phenomenally efficient at performing mental math.

The abacus is a great example of what we might call a mental tool; that is, a tool that helps us do mental work. Vygotsky (1978) proposed that such tools (he referred to them as *signs*) were the key to the development of our capacity to think. In fact, he viewed them as the very essence of thought itself. This is the metaphorical leap he made. Just as tools were central to the development of humans as a species and the development of human society, so *mental* tools are central to the development of individual cognition. In fact, Vygotsky believed the modern mind only existed *because* of such tools.

To make sense of this point, let's back up and talk more about physical work and physical tools. Vygotsky (1978) referred to any work with a tool as mediated activity. The tool mediates between us and the environment, transforming the nature of the work. Nearly all human work is mediated by the use of tools. This even applies to activities we do not typically refer to as "work." Take skiing as an example. This activity, like many activities, is not possible without a particular set of tools. Not only are the tools important to the activity, but the nature of the activity is tied to the nature of the tools.

Figure 7.2 illustrates different kinds of ski gear. Cross-country (aka Nordic) ski gear was invented first. Such gear generally involves a flexible shoe attached at the toe to a long, skinny, and light ski. Nordic gear allows individuals to traverse snowy terrain they could not traverse otherwise; at least, not without much difficulty. The advantage of Nordic gear over snowshoes is that it allows one to glide along more efficiently once a trail is made.

However, going downhill on Nordic gear is a bit of an adventure to say the least. Consequently, innovative skiers began adapting the gear. They developed stiffer boots, fatter skis, and bindings that more securely attached the boot to the ski but still left the heel free to rise up and down. These new tools transformed skiing. Now, by learning the telemark technique (dropping the inside knee to make a turn), skiers could comfortably ski downhill. Many backcountry skiers today[2] use such equipment to get away from crowded resorts and experience untracked powder runs in the wilderness. These are the people who have bumper stickers reading, "Free the Heel and Ski Real" or "Drop the Knee and Ski Free." Or they are people like me who say, "I dropped the knee and can't get up."

---

[2] Actually, backcountry gear of the type I am describing is becoming more and more rare. Now it seems everyone uses alpine touring gear.

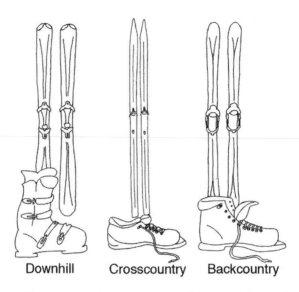

Downhill   Crosscountry   Backcountry

FIGURE 7.2.   Different types of Ski Gear. (Artwork by McKinley Pugh.)

Additional innovations led to the development of downhill (aka Alpine) gear. Such gear involves yet fatter and heavier skis, stiff plastic boots, and bindings that lock in both the toe and heel of the boot. These new tools further transformed the activity by providing far more stability and security to downhill skiing. Now you see kids who can barely walk learning to ski, teenagers doing all sorts of tricks, and "free skiers" descending nearly vertical faces of alpine peaks. The gear changed everything.

The point is that tools mediate the nature of our physical activities. Different tools open new possibilities and constrain others. Vygotsky proposed that nearly all mental activity is likewise mediated by tools, and the nature and quality of our mental activity is dependent on the nature and quality of the mental tools. This is worth repeating. *The nature and quality of our mental activity is dependent on the nature and quality of our mental tools.*

For example, nearly all our mathematical reasoning is mediated by some mental tool. The abacus is a concrete example of a tool that can mediate mathematical problem solving, but it is certainly not the only tool. You probably added the five 3-digit numbers using an algorithm you were taught in school. This algorithm, like all algorithms, is another mental tool created by a prior society and culture. You internalized it, and now it mediates your mathematical reasoning. The algorithm is a powerful tool for completing certain kinds of math problems, but a mental image of an abacus is an even more powerful tool for performing mental math. The nature and quality of the math you do is tied to the mental tools you have acquired. In fact, without any mental tools, it is doubtful you could do math at all.

The Man Without Words

Now let us turn our attention to the mother of all mental tools: language. That's right, language itself is not only a mental tool, but *the* fundamental mental tool. Vygotsky (1986) proposed that we first learn to use language in interaction with other people. Then we gradually internalize language and use it with ourselves. That is, external speech becomes inner speech, and it is this moment, when we learn to speak to ourselves, that the most profound development in thought takes place. Thought, as we know it, comes into existence.

If you doubt him, then try having a deep thought without using language. Try having *any* thought without using language. How did it go? It is difficult to even conceive of what thought is like without language. But we can gain some insights by studying individuals who grew up without language. Individuals like Ildefonso.

In her book, *A Man Without Words*, Susan Schaller (1991) describes her experience of meeting Ildefonso (a pseudonym) and helping him learn language. Schaller first met Ildefonso in a reading skills class for deaf students at a community college. She was there largely by mistake. She had signed up for work as a sign language interpreter and was sent to this classroom, but the teacher and aid were both fluent in sign. As Schaller soon realized, a number of the students were there by mistake, too. They did not just lack reading skills. They lacked language all together.

Ildefonso was one of these individuals. He was 27 years old and was raised in southern Mexico without any exposure to education or sign language. His uncle had registered him for the class. Schaller sat down with Ildefonso and tried to interact using sign. He simply copied back the movements displayed with no recognition that such movements meant anything. She left frustrated and overwhelmed. How could you teach someone who had no language, no recognition that there *is* such a thing as language?

Schaller spent the next week patiently trying to convey the idea that a thing can be represented by a symbol. This idea is so fundamental to our thinking that it is hard to imagine its absence. Yet, to someone without language, the very idea of naming objects has not yet developed. Schaller tried to teach this idea by using gesture and mime to connect signs with objects. She began by taking Ildefonso outside and gestured toward a tree and then signing "tree." She handled a leaf, patted the tree, and nodded alternatively between her hand signing "tree" and the actual tree. Ildefonso copied the sign but with no recognition that the hand motions meant anything.

For the next five days, Schaller focused on connecting the symbol "cat" to the object cat. In every possible combination, Schaller signed "cat," finger-spelled "cat," wrote "cat," acted like a cat, pointed to a picture of a cat, and mimed petting a cat, all the while trying to get Ildefonso to make that crucial cognitive leap;

to understand that these actions referenced the same thing. However, Ildefonso continued to merely mimic Schaller's actions.

Out of frustration, Schaller decided to ignore him. This was actually quite a clever move. She began miming both the role of the teacher and the student. As a teacher, she would go through her regular routines of signing "cat," petting an imaginary cat, pointing to the word cat, and so on. Then she would sit down and act out being a student. First acting confused and then nodding in understanding while pointing to the word cat, pointing to her head, and stroking an imaginary cat. She spent most the day miming this teacher-student "cat" routine in every possible variation.

The next day, at Ildefonso's urging, she continued with it. Over and over. Cat after cat. Then, in mid-mime, something clicked in Ildefonso's mind. Schaller writes,

> Suddenly he sat up, straight and rigid, his head back and his chin pointing forward. The whites of his eyes expanded as if in terror. He looked like a wild horse pulling back, testing every muscle before making a powerful lunge over a canyon's edge. My body and arms froze in the mime-and-sign dance that I had played over and over for an eternity. I stood motionless in front of the streaked *cat*, petted beyond recognition for the fiftieth time, and I witnessed Ildefonso's emancipation. He broke through. He understood....Yes c-a-t *mean* something. And the cat-meaning in one head can join the cat-meaning in another's head just by tossing out a *cat*. (1991, p. 44)

Ildefonso looked eagerly around at the objects in the room. He slapped his hands on the table, and Schaller signed back "table." He slapped his book, and she signed "book." He demanded the signs for more objects, and Schaller gave them. What happened next is both revealing and heartbreaking. Ildefonso suddenly turned pale. He collapsed on the table. He began to weep.

Imagine what it would be like to suddenly realize that a whole world of meaning and human connection existed. Yet you had missed out on this world your whole life. You had been locked in a world of incomprehension and isolation. Would you not weep too? Schaller writes,

> Welcome to my world, Ildefonso...Let me show you all the miracles accomplished with symbols...I will show you how to bathe in the swirling, magical river called Language. You can swim anywhere, meet anyone and anything, or just float on one of those lovely names. Let me open the door to this world that refused to let you in. (p. 45)

Full use and comprehension of language did not come in a flash for Ildefonso. Rather, this first "awakening" was merely the realization of language. The insight that such a thing existed. Over the next four months, Schaller worked painstakingly with Ildefonso to help him acquire language. It was often a slow and laborious process with many moments of confusion and frustration. But slowly he began to learn language and in doing so, internalized many of the mental tools and subsequent ways of thinking that you and I take for granted. One illustrative example is Ildefonso's development of an understanding of time.

It seems we are born with a general sense of time, but units of time (seconds, minutes, hours, days, weeks, months, years, decades, centuries, millennia, and so on) are powerful mental tools that come to mediate our thinking. Ildefonso had no such mediated thinking in relation to time. Schaller did not know how Ildefonso knew when to come to class and, indeed, suspected that he had shown up for class on weekends only to be bewildered as to why no one else was there.

Schaller began the arduous process of helping Ildefonso grasp the abstract concept of time. She mimed the sun going across the sky and connected this to the sign for day. She mimed growing up and connected this to counting years. On and on she went for a few weeks, but Ildefonso did not seem to grasp the idea of counting time or see the significance of doing so.

Then one day there was a party in class. Schaller signed that it was a birthday party and went through her mime-and-dance routine to explain that the day, month, and year of a person's birth is noted and celebrated each year. Ildefonso finally understood and accepted the practice of counting time as they then began counting down the days until Ildefonso's birthday, which was in a few weeks. He became more and more excited as the day approached.

If you think about it, this must have been the first time he ever anticipated the approach of an event in a mediated way. The first time he ever thought about an event as occurring at a particular point in a system of time, and the first time he could track his progress toward that point. The class threw Ildefonso a surprise birthday party. This was his first real birthday party. The first time he understood that it was a celebration of his birth—a birth that occurred at particular point in time that could be defined by a date. For a present, the class gave Ildefonso a watch.

By the end of the semester, Ildefonso had developed basic language. His vocabulary was limited and communication was still difficult, but the basic elements of language had taken root. He graduated from the class, and Schaller moved to the East coast. After seven years, she returned to California and wanted to reconnect with Ildefonso.

After months of searching, she tracked him down. A joyous meeting ensued, and Schaller was thrilled to see Ildefonso signing confidently and fluidly. Other meetings followed, and Schaller tried to get Ildefonso to talk about his life before language. What was it like to not have language? What was it like to think without language? Ildefonso never answered these questions directly. Instead, he took Schaller to meet some old friends who also lacked language.

The friends communicated almost exclusively through miming particular experiences, and they lacked the kind of cognitive functioning that Ildefonso now possessed. For them, Ildefonso had become an awe-inspiring figure. Schaller writes, "His leap to language dumbfounded them.... They considered him a genius and treated him with great respect. He had become the leader of the languageless clan" (pp. 184–185).

For Ildefonso, it was very important that Schaller understand this languageless clan; he wanted her to understand how they functioned, how they communicated, how they *were*. Because by understanding them, she could understand him—the pre-language Ildefonso. Schaller described the experience in this way:

> [Ildefonso's] eyes leaped back and forth from my eyes to the storytellers, measuring my response and their performance. "See? See? Did you see that? Look!" He constantly directed my gaze to make sure I didn't miss a movement. He had to answer all those unanswerable questions I had asked years before. He wanted me to know who he had been, how he had lived, and his only experience with tribal life, with community. He knew who he was now and knew that what he had learned could not be appreciated without knowledge of where he had started. (p. 188)

On a WNYC (2010) Radiolab program, Schaller explained that two years after this experience, she ran into Ildefonso and again tried to get him to directly talk about what it was like to not have language. She commented that he was again evasive and then added, "But the interesting thing that he said was he can't even *think* that way anymore. He said he can't think the way he used to think." When Schaller pushed him to give some ideas of what it was like, he responded, "I don't know. I don't remember."

Such is the power of language as a mental tool. It so transforms thinking that prior thinking is no longer possible. It cannot even be recalled to memory.

In Vygotsky's view, knowledge and thinking cannot be separated from the mental tools of a society. This is one way learning can be seen as "situated" in society and in the cultural practices of society, and why Vygotsky is considered a pioneer of the situated learning perspective (chapter 8). In fact, if we take his ideas seriously, we can even begin to question the degree to which independent thought exists.

IMPLICATIONS

Innate Intelligence Is Over-rated

We regard innate intelligence very highly in our society. We revel in fictional characters such as Sherlock Holmes and historical figures such as Einstein. Such individuals are seen as being infinitely smarter than the rest of us on some hard-wired level. Maybe they are. But then again, maybe it is not so simple. Maybe it is all about the tools.

Tools often render innate ability irrelevant. Say we had a 5'6" 110 lb. fellow and a 6'4" 260 lb. guy both trying to move a large stone. Innate physical ability makes a large difference when they are trying to move it with their own bodies. But once this activity becomes mediated, that is, once we introduce tools, then the importance of innate physical ability diminishes. In fact, if the tool involved is a bulldozer, then innate physical ability becomes irrelevant. Does this same logic apply to mental work and mental tools?

It likely does to some degree. Success on cognitive tasks has a lot more to do with the mental tools an individual possesses than the innate intelligence of that individual. Malcolm Gladwell (2008) illustrates this point quite effectively in his book *Outliers: The Story of Success*. In that book, he reports on a famous study conducted by Lewis Terman.

In 1921, Terman decided to study the effects of genius-level intelligence on life functioning and success. He started by identifying a sample of elementary school children with genius level IQs. He found 1,470 and followed them through adulthood. In a truly astonishing finding, Terman discovered that the average level of success of the "Termites," as they were called, was, well, average. Some were highly successful, but many were not.

These were devastating results for Terman. He had expected them all to become brilliant scientists, famous politicians, renowned physicians, and the like. Instead, they were not that different from an average group. Gladwell (2008) writes,

> In a devastating critique, the sociologist Pitirim Sorokin once showed that if Terman had simply put together a randomly selected group of children from the same kinds of family backgrounds as the Termites—and dispensed with IQs altogether—he would have ended up with a group doing almost as many impressive things as his painstakingly selected group of geniuses. (p. 90)

Intelligence, at least a represented by IQ, seemed to count for little.

To further illustrate this point, Gladwell presents the story of Chris Langan, who has an IQ between 195 and 210. To give you some perspective, an IQ of 100 is average. Above 135 is the top 1%. Above 140 is genius-level intelligence. Albert Einstein, Stephen Hawking, and Bill Gates all had IQs of 160. In fact, Langan's IQ is one of the highest ever recorded. He is truly one in a million, maybe one in a billion. So, what has all this innate intelligence got Langan? Not much in terms of our typical measures of success.

Langan went to college with high hopes but struggled with the logistics and eventually dropped out. He found work at a bar and became known as the world's smartest bouncer. Currently he owns and runs a horse ranch. He still writes about science and philosophy and is working on a theory of the relationship between the mind and reality. However, to date, his work and theories have not been well received by other scientists and philosophers. Perhaps they will be someday, but it seems more likely that his work and theories simply are not up to the standards of the scholarly community.

Isaac Newton famously proclaimed, "If I have seen further it is only by standing on the shoulders of giants." By this he meant that he did not see himself as an intellectual giant. Instead, he believed he was simply building on the ideas laid down by others. In other words, he internalized the mental tools constructed by his predecessors and used them to build new tools.

It seems Langan missed the opportunity to be mentored by the leading minds of our generation and guided through a process of acquiring the great mental tools of the past. He is as the world's mightiest warrior, armed with a few twigs while his opponents wield swords, spears, and rocket launchers.

Cultural Mismatches Impede Learning

In the Terman study, the only reliable predictor of success among the geniuses was family income. Why? Psychologists today are apt to explain the discrepancy in terms of cultural capital.

Definitions of cultural capital can get complex (see Bourdieu, 1986, for the original conceptualization), but it is generally defined as the more informal knowledge and skills needed to be successful in society. It can include such things as knowledge of how to navigate the educational system or knowing when you have a voice and how to use this voice. Individuals from privileged positions in society have greater opportunity to internalize such knowledge and skills. Disadvantaged individuals often struggle in education or work because they lack such opportunities, and these informal knowledge and skills are not explicitly taught.

Chris Langan, for example, grew up in very poor circumstances and lacked the cultural capital of many of his peers. When he attended college, he struggled simply because he lacked knowledge of available options when barriers arose, and didn't know he had a voice in the system. I have to admit, sometimes I feel sick when I think about Langan's (and society's) lost opportunity all because of such seemingly insignificant knowledge.

From a Vygotskian perspective, we could say that cultural capital consists of informal mental tools that help us do the work of negotiating social situations and societal structures. Disadvantaged children often lack the requisite mental tools for being successful in critical societal structures. However, it would be a mistake to say these children have a *deficiency* of mental tools. They internalize the mental tools critical to their local societal structures. The problem is the potential *mismatch* between the mental tools needed for participating in these local societal structures and those needed for participating in mainstream societal structures. We refer to this situation as a cultural mismatch. A parable may help clarify the meaning of cultural mismatch.

The Parable of the Choppers

Jacques and Cleaver are both skilled at a fundamental human competency: chopping things up. Jacques is an up-and-coming chef and Cleaver is a burgeoning lumberjack. Both developed their skills through their cultural experience. Jacques' parents own a restaurant, and he grew up cooking things. Cleaver's parents own a lumber mill, and he grew up logging.

Due to a strange set of circumstances involving a girl, Jacques moved to Cleaver's hometown of Smithers in British Columbia, Canada. There, the mayor decided that at least two years of college should be mandatory for all Smithersites, so Jacques and Cleaver both enrolled in the local school, Paul Bunyan Community College.

In their first class, both Jacques and Cleaver were asked to carve benches out of logs with a chainsaw. Cleaver was quickly labeled a gifted student while Jacques was labeled a remedial student with a learning disability and an attitude problem.

In the above parable, both individuals have cutting skills. But only one has skills that match those required by the educational setting. This is a common occurrence in education, and such cultural mismatches help explain why disadvantaged students often struggle and become frustrated with school.

Consider the following situation documented by Shirley Brice Heath (1982; 1983). Teachers at a school in North Carolina were frustrated by the lack of engagement in learning activities by students from Trackton (pseudonym), a rural, black community. These teachers wrote evaluations like the following:

"Doesn't seem to know how to answer a simple, direct question."

"I would almost think some of them have a hearing problem; it is as through they don't hear me ask a question. I get blank stares to my questions."

"The simplest questions are the ones they can't answer in the classroom; yet on the playground they can explain a rule for a ball game or describe a particular kind of bait with no problem. Therefore, I know they can't be as dumb as they seem in my class." (Heath, 1983, pp. 268–269)

On the other hand, parents of these children made comments such as these:

"Miss Davis, she complain 'bout Ned not answerin' back. He says she asks dumb questions she already know about."

"My kid, he too scared to talk, 'cause nobody play by the rules he know. At home I can't shut him up." (Heath, 1982, p. 107)

What's going on here? To understand, we have to look at language use in Trackton and in school; particularly the use of questioning.

Heath studied language use within the Trackton community and found that adults did not typically interact with children as conversation partners. Consequently, they did not develop questions especially geared for children, such as questions that tested children's knowledge of the world or allowed them to show off their knowledge of the world. As one parent put it, "We don't talk to our chil'rn like you folks do. We don't ask 'em 'bout colors, names, 'n things" (p. 109).

Adults in Trackton almost never asked children rhetorical questions; that is, questions in which the adult knows the right answer and expects the child to recite it. Instead, they commonly used analogy and comparison questions with children. Questions like, "What's dat like?" or "Who he actin' like?" Children were not expected to guess the adult's answer to such questions and respond accordingly.

Instead, they were simply being prompted to make a comparison. This is the type of question children in Trackton learned to ask and answer. This is the mental tool that they internalized for negotiating and making sense of the world.

Now consider school. What kinds of questions are used there? Well, rhetorical questions tend to dominate. What color is this? What do we call this shape? What is two plus two? Who was our first president? Children in Trackton have no experience with this type of question.

Now recall one of the teachers' comments, "The simplest questions are the ones they can't answer in the classroom." Well, of course they can't! From a Trackton student's perspective, it *makes no sense* to ask a question to which you already know the answer. Consider this parent's comments again: "He says she asks dumb questions she already knows about." Such questions seem so nonsensical that the Trackton students believed something else must be going on. The teacher must be playing some sort of game to which the rules were a mystery. As the second parent stated, "My kid, he too scared to talk, 'cause nobody play by the rules he know."

The cultural mismatch between the school and the Trackton students extended beyond just questions. It included other forms of language use (e.g., storytelling) and understanding of "polite" behavior. Together, these cultural mismatches made it hard for Trackton students to be successful in school.

Thankfully, a number of teachers became aware of these cultural mismatches through Heath's research, and began building bridges to the Trackton students' ways of using language and other cultural actions. They found ways for the students to use their familiar mental tools. By doing so, they helped integrate the students into the school community, school activities, and taught them what it means to "do schooling." Suddenly, the kids who "can't be as dumb as they seem in my class" were not.

Learning Is a Process of Enculturation

In Vygotsky's model of learning, we naturally internalize mental tools as we participate in social and cultural activities. We "grow into the intellectual life" of those around us (Vygotsky, 1978, p. 88). Learning, we might say, is a process of enculturation.

What does it mean to be enculturated? Well, think about your high school experience. You likely became a member of a particular group or clique and learned certain ways of acting, dressing, and socializing simply through your participation as a member of the group. Take my high school experience as an example. After a brief foray into the "new wave" clique (this was the '80s, please do not look up my freshman yearbook picture), I became part a group later referred to as the "granolas." We all had a common interest in the outdoors, and through our interactions with the larger outdoor-focused, hippie culture, we developed common ways of acting, dressing, and thinking.

We advocated independent thinking, but we all looked the same in our tie-dye or Patagonia clothing. We all wore hiking boots or Teva sandals and had big mops of hair. Apparently, we even walked the same. My wife, who went to the same school but wisely kept her distance, tells me we all walked stooped over carrying big backpacks and we "bounced" as we walked, causing our mop of hair to float up and down with each step. We hung out in the hall playing hacky sack, listening to the Grateful Dead, and talking about the virtues of being a non-conformist (while nodding in unison). There was never a discussion or decision about how to act, how to look, or how to think. It simply happened as we came to participate in a particular culture.

This is what it means to become enculturated. We "grow into" ways of being simply through our participation in particular cultures or communities. We naturally internalize mental tools in the same way. That is, through our participation in social and cultural activities. However, school learning is often disconnected from such participation.

To address this problem, scholars have advocated modeling school instruction after real-world apprenticeships (e.g., Brown, Collins, & Duguid, 1989; Lave & Wenger, 1991). An apprenticeship is a formalized model of learning through enculturation. You learn through participating in and becoming a part of a particular cultural activity (e.g., blacksmithing, painting).

The apprenticeship model of learning has a few readily definable characteristics. Some type of "master" models correct action and erects scaffolding, such as support and guidance, for the apprentice. The scaffolding is gradually removed as the apprentice gains competence. There is a progression from peripheral involvement in the skill (e.g., working the bellows for the blacksmith) to the more central aspects (e.g., creating a horseshoe). Finally, all the learning is done in the context of the real-world activity.

These characteristics have been employed in the design of "cognitive" apprenticeships. That is, apprenticeships designed to enculturate students into particular ways of thinking about content (e.g., particular ways of scientific thinking) or in the development of particular cognitive skills (e.g., reading comprehension).

A prominent example of a cognitive apprenticeship is reciprocal teaching (Palincsar & Brown, 1984). Reciprocal teaching is a small-group instruction model designed to boost reading comprehension. The developers, Ann Marie Palincsar and Ann Brown, were perplexed by kids who could verbally read text just fine but failed to comprehend what they read. Palincsar and Brown discovered that students with poor comprehension lacked basic reflective skills. You can think of these skills as the mental tools needed to do the work of comprehending text. Such tools include making predictions based on the text, seeking clarification when something does not make sense, asking questions of the text, and summarizing the text. Most of us use these tools naturally, but students with poor comprehension do not.

Teaching such tools directly in a decontextualized manner is typically not effective, so Palincsar and Brown sought an alternative. They decided to draw on Vygotsky's theory and provide an apprenticeship-type environment that enculturated the students into using these skills. Specifically, they chose to create a reading environment that involved modeling and scaffolding of the comprehension tools, transfer of responsibility to students, and learning in the context of meaningful reading activity. It worked phenomenally well. Within a couple weeks, students who were 2 ½ years below grade level on reading comprehension suddenly achieved grade level.

So what does reciprocal teaching look like? Imagine a group of five students and one teacher sitting together in a circle working on reading a passage of text. Initially, the teacher might model reading comprehension strategies. For example, the teacher might model making predictions by pointing to the title and saying something like, "This first sentence mentions lightning and 'understanding the mystery' so I predict that this passage is going to give me information about what causes lightning."

In addition to modeling, the teacher will assign students to take responsibility for using the strategies. For example, she might ask, "Keecham, could you give us a summary of what we just read?" Initially, students poor at reading comprehension are likely to be terrible at using these skills. They make predictions that do not follow from the text, they ask questions that are only loosely connected to the text, and they provide summaries that ignore significant parts of the text. But the teacher would carefully scaffold the students' efforts and help them use the strategies productively.

For instance, the teacher might scaffold use of the predicting strategy by saying, "OK Arianna. I noticed the title mentions dogs and your prediction is a story about dogs, but let's look at the title again. What else is mentioned? How might that help us predict what the passage is going to be about?" The teacher and student (and possibly other students) would then interact until an acceptable prediction was constructed.

Over the course of a couple weeks, the dynamics of the group would change such that students take on more and more responsibility for using the skills, and the teacher fades out her support. Eventually, the group gets to the point where the support of the teacher is no longer needed. On their own, they can apply the skills effectively. At this point, something wonderful happens. The students start to comprehend what they read—even when they are not in the reciprocal teaching group. Through their participation in the group, they have come to internalize the mental tools needed to comprehend what one reads.

It would be incorrect to say that all learning occurs through a process of enculturation. However, it is an important learning process, especially for acquiring the vital mental tools of our culture such as language. And it is a process often neglected in school.

Do We Even Have an Individual Mind?

If you take the *mind as cultural tools* perspective seriously, then it leads to the conclusion that our very thought and intelligence is not our own. Instead, it is a product of history and culture. Crazy idea you say? Well, hear me out.

If nearly all our capacity to engage in sophisticated mental work comes from internalizing mental tools—tools constructed by societies both modern and ancient—then what intelligence can we really claim as being our own? If we cannot even do basic math without the aid of cultural tools, can we claim that our mathematical intelligence is our own? If we cannot think the same without language, can we claim our thoughts as our own? I do not know that we can, and this is a humbling realization.

We probably do not realize or acknowledge the degree to which our thoughts and intelligence are shaped and determined by our mental tools. Take former Minnesota governor Jesse Ventura's statement as an example. He made waves in a 1999 interview when he said, "Organized religion is a sham and crutch for the weak-minded." The implication, as picked up and championed by others such as comedian Bill Maher, was that people who cannot think for themselves about moral situations need religion to tell them what to think.

But wait a second. Can we think for ourselves about moral situations? Is such a thing even possible? Can we think for ourselves, *period*? If we take seriously the idea that our capacity to think is a consequence of internalizing the mental tools constructed by society, then the answer may be no.

Think about it this way. If Ventura said math algorithms are a crutch for the weak-minded, you would say he is crazy. You would say such algorithms are the very essence with which we reason mathematically. And you would be correct. This same principle applies to all our reasoning, whether it is reasoning about science, politics, or morality.

Without religion or other philosophies of values, we would have no tools with which to reason about moral situations. Concepts such as respect, equality, fairness, and forgiveness are the mental tools that allow us to even conceive of a moral situation. Without such constructs, our sense of morality is like pre-language Ildefonso's sense of time—an innate impression that is vague and unfulfilled.

Mental tools, whether they be religious constructs or mathematical principles, are not for the weak-minded; they bring into existence the mind itself! This is why Vygotsky titled one of his books Mind in Society. The mind literally exists as a function of society.

Moreover, because these mental tools constitute our reasoning, they shape our reasoning. We cannot separate ourselves from them. We reason about moral situations in terms of respect and equality because these are the tools we have been given. Our reasoning would be different if we had a different set of tools. We cannot engage in thinking independent of these tools. In this sense, there is no true independence of thought. No true thinking for one's self. At least, that is where my wholly original and independent thinking leads me.

REFERENCES

Bourdieu, P. (1986). The forms of capital. In J. Richardson (Ed.), *Handbook of theory and research for the sociology of education* (pp. 241–258). New York, NY: Greenwood.

Brown, J. S., Collins, A., & Duguid, P. (1989). Situated cognition and the culture of learning. *Educational Researcher, 18*(1), 32–42. doi:10.3102/0013189X018001032

Gladwell, M. (2008). *Outliers: The story of success.* London, UK: Allen Lane.

Heath, S. B. (1982). Questioning at home and at school: A comparative study. In G. Spindler (Ed.), *Doing the ethnography of schooling* (pp. 102–131). New York: Holt, Rinehart and Winston.

Heath, S. B. (1983). *Ways with words: Language, life and work in communities and classrooms.* New York, NY: Cambridge.

Langham, D. (1994). The common place MOO: Orality and literacy in virtual reality. *Computer-Mediated Communication Magazine, 1*(3), 7.

Lave, J., & Wenger, E. (1991). *Situated learning: Legitimate peripheral participation.* Cambridge, MA: Cambridge University Press.

Palincsar, A. S., & Brown, A. L. (1984). Reciprocal teaching of comprehension-fostering and comprehension-monitoring activities. *Cognition and Instruction, 1*, 117–175. doi:10.1207/s1532690xci0102_1

Prawat, R. S. (2000). Dewey meets the "Mozart of psychology" in Moscow: The untold story. *American Educational Research Journal, 37*, 663–696. doi:10.3102/00028312037003663

Schaller, S. (1991). *A man without words.* New York, NY: Summit Books.

Stigler, J. W. (1984). "Mental abacus": The effect of abacus training on Chinese children's mental calculation. *Cognitive Psychology, 16*, 145–176. doi:10.1016/0010-0285(84)90006-9

Vygotsky, L. (1978). *Mind in society: The development of higher psychological processes.* Cambridge, MA: Harvard University Press.

Vygotsky, L. (1986). *Thought and language* (A. Kozulin, trans.). Cambridge, MA: MIT Press.

WNYC. (2010, August 9). *Radiolab: Words.* Retrieved 2011-10-23 from http://www.radiolab.org/series/podcasts.

CHAPTER 8

LEARNING AS COCKROACH OR PANDA BEAR

Disclaimer: The situative perspective is conceptualized in different ways by different people, and some of these conceptualizations get quite esoteric. I am sure I will not do justice to some of these conceptualizations.

Vygotsky's ideas helped give rise to the situative perspective. This perspective takes the position that learning is grounded in social and cultural situations. In a landmark paper, Brown, Collins, & Duguid (1989) put it this way,

> The activity in which knowledge is developed and deployed, it is now argued, is not separable from or ancillary to learning and cognition. Nor is it neutral. Rather, it is an integral part of what is learned. Situations might be said to co-produce knowledge through activity. Learning and cognition, it is now possible to argue, are fundamentally situated. (p. 32)

Clear? No? Perhaps this will help, "Situativity focuses primarily at the level of interactive systems that include individuals as participants, interacting with each other and with material and representational systems" (Greeno, 1997, p. 7).

One more definition for good measure:

Computers, Cockroaches, and Ecosystems: Understanding Learning through Metaphor, pages 127–139.

The situative perspective holds that learning is embodied in social and cultural communities of practice and grounded in the affordances and constraints of situated action in which interdependence and intersubjectivity develop within trajectories of participation in accordance with participatory structures and attunement and effectivities on the part of agents contextualized in symbolic and semiotic representational systems within discourse communities situated against a sociocultural milieu.

Ok, I made that last one up. My point is that the words and ideas comprising the situated learning perspective are so unfamiliar and abstract that individuals struggle to understand the theory. I find it helpful to make sense of it in terms of cockroaches and panda bears. It sounds strange, but hear me out.

Suppose we have a pair of naïve biology students sent out to study the relationship between animals and their environments. One is given the pleasurable task of studying panda bears, and the other, who must have been a troublemaker, is assigned to research cockroaches. After years of field study, the two come back and give their reports. The cockroach scholar takes the stage first and commences, "The relationship between the cockroach and its environment is fairly loose. Cockroaches can survive in a wide variety of environments ranging from the heart of the Amazon jungle to the space under your refrigerator. They have no precise diet and can survive off just about anything, including the glue on the back of a stamp. If the environment turns watery, they can survive underwater for up to half an hour. If the environment drops below freezing, some just freeze and then thaw out when the temperature warms up. They can survive much higher levels of radiation than human beings. Quite frankly, there seem to be very few limits to the environments in which cockroaches can survive and thrive. Thus, based on my research, I must conclude that animals are generally context-free. They can freely move between many different environments and successfully adapt." With this, he sits down and begins playing with his new pet, a three-inch Madagascar hissing cockroach.

The panda scholar then takes the stage sporting a "Save the Panda" cap and proceeds to contradict the basic premises of the cockroach scholar. "According to my research, we must conclude that animals are tightly bound to a particular environment. The panda only survives in a few mountain ranges in central China. There, it is restricted to bamboo forests between about 1,600 and 3,200 meters in elevation. These forests need to be at least one hundred years old with large felled trees and at least two species of bamboo. In addition, a breeding pair requires at least 7,500 acres of habitat, and a healthy population requires a much larger area connected by bamboo corridors. Any variation from this environment, and the panda population will die off. In fact, they already are dying off because the necessary habitat keeps getting smaller and smaller." At this, our panda scholars becomes a bit chocked up, mumbles something about World Wildlife Fund donation forms in the lobby, and ambles back to her seat.

So are animals generally context-free as our cockroach scholar suggests or context-bound as our panda scholar believes? Well, obviously it depends on your perspective and the animals you study. The same can be said of learning, with the situative perspective representing the more context-bound perspective—sort of. As always, it is a bit more complex than that.

MAKING SENSE OF THE METAPHOR

In general, the cognitive and constructivist perspectives assume that learning is, or at least can be, like the cockroach. That is, they suggest skills and knowledge can exist apart from specific learning environments. They focus on the nature of these skills and knowledge, and how they can be applied across many different contexts. In contrast, situative scholars operate on the assumption that learning is, like the panda, tightly bound to a particular context. To understand the panda, you have to study the whole habitat in which it lives. Likewise, to understand learning, you have to study its whole social, cultural, and situational context.

Everyday Learning

I could be wrong, but I believe this alternative approach was, at least partially, a result of the kind of learning situations studied. The situative perspective largely grew out of studies of learning in everyday contexts. Such learning, like the panda, often displays a context-bound nature. For example, Scribner (1984) studied the mathematical practices of dairy workers as they completed such tasks as filling milk orders and taking inventory. She found that their mathematical reasoning could not be separated from the physical context of the facility. The workers used their knowledge of the milk crates and of physical space in the facility to do their mathematical reasoning.

For instance, a preloader reported completing an order through visualization instead of counting, "I knew the case I was looking at had ten out of it, and I only wanted eight, so I just added two…I don't never count when I'm making the order. I do it visual, a visual thing, you know" (p. 26). Similarly, other workers took inventory, in part, by visualizing the space occupied by a certain number of cases and combining this with their knowledge of cartons per case. The mathematical practices they used were bound to this particular context.

Similarly, Lave, Murtaugh, and de la Rocha (1984) studied the mathematical practices of experienced shoppers in the grocery story and found that grocery store math was often very different from school math. The math used in the grocery store was unique to the goals, purposes, symbol systems, and physical features of that setting. They concluded that the setting and the mathematical activity create each other and cannot be understood separately. Just as the panda is tightly bound to a particular environmental context, so much of everyday learning is tightly bound to specific contexts. In this sense, the learning is situated in a particular context.

However, there is a larger point stemming from the situative perspective. Over time, the emphasis within the situative perspective shifted from a focus on the context-bound nature of learning to a focus on understanding learning—all learning—in relation to its context. Indeed, I am sure I have raised the ire of situative scholars everywhere simply by using the language of "context-bound" learning. They would emphasize that the situative perspective does not claim all knowledge is context-bound. Rather the perspective claims this is the wrong way of talking about learning (Greeno, 1997).

Think about it this way: even the cockroach, which can move between and adapt to many different contexts, always exists within *some* context. Talking exclusively about individual survival characteristics possessed by the cockroach neglects the point that such characteristics only have significance within some context, and that survival is an interplay between individual and context. For these reasons, situative scholars have steered away from talking about learning in terms of knowledge possessed by the individual and presumed to exist apart from context. Instead, they talk about and study learning as participation in cultural activity (which is similar to studying survival of organisms in environments) (Greeno, Collins, & Resnick, 1996; Lave & Wenger, 1991; Rogoff, 1993). From this perspective, the role of context is always taken into consideration.

To better make sense of this idea, we can return to the ecosystem metaphor (chapter 6) and use it slightly differently. Instead of viewing ideas in the mind as the ecosystem within which individual ideas must be considered, we can view context as the ecosystem within which individual learners must be considered. That is, we can study learning as embedded in a dynamic ecosystem involving settings, activities, and multiple layers of societal structures (e.g., immediate family, local community, broader culture). To understand any learning, we need to study it in relation to this larger context. Increasingly, this larger context itself has become the unit of analysis (i.e., the object of study). That is, instead of studying the learning of individuals and considering how their learning might be impacted by other people or the environment, the focus has shifted to studying the dynamics of the ecosystem itself. For example, studying the dynamics of a learning community as opposed to individual learning processes or the functioning of a team instead of individual player skills.

Jocks and Burnouts

Eckert (1989) studied learning by focusing on the "ecosystem" of student peer groups and local neighborhood communities. At the school she studied, there were two dominant peer groups. One group hung out in the courtyard, of which Eckert provides this description:

> There are boys wearing flared or bell-bottomed jeans, running shoes, rock concert T-shirts, parkas, jean jackets. A few have chains attaching their wallets to a belt loop…
> Many have long hair…hold cigarettes in their mouths…There are girls with virtually the same clothes, a number with long straight hair, darkly made-up eyes…hold-

ing cigarettes before them between extended fingers…Occasionally a hit changes hands, or a joint passes through the group. (p. 1)

These were the Burnouts or "Jells" (short for Jello Brains). The opposing group hung out in the cafeteria, which Eckert described as an area that,

roars with conversation, eyes dart across the surrounding crowd, shouts and greetings fly between groups. These people are wearing slacks or jeans with the currently more fashionable pegged or straight-legged cut…Many sport designer labels, carefully feathered hairdos [this was the 80s after all], and perfectly made-up pastel faces…Postures are straight and open, faces are smiling. The hall is as crowded and agitated as the courtyard is spacious and subdued. (p. 1)

This group was the Jocks, which is somewhat of a misnomer as athletics was not the defining characteristic. Rather this group could be considered the popular or conformist group while the Burnouts represented the anti-establishment group. Nearly all schools have variations of these groups.

Eckert found that students' engagement in school was largely a function of the social group to which they belonged. The Jocks were defined by a school-oriented attitude. One student explained that a Jock is,

Someone who gets into school, who does her homework, who, uh, goes to all the activities, who's in concert choir, who has her whole days surrounded by school. You know, "tonight I'm gong go to concert choir practice and today maybe I'll go watch track, and then early this morning maybe, oh, I'll go help a teacher or something." (p. 1)

The Burnouts were defined by their opposition to school. For example, one girl explained that she didn't work on yearbook, despite her interest, because only Jocks worked on yearbook. She was a Burnout and the Burnouts didn't consider it cool to do school activities (p. 88). Consequently, students who identified themselves as part of the Jock crowd increasingly identified with the mission of the school and became engaged in school, including academic engagement. Those who were part of the Burnouts did the opposite.

It might be tempting to assume that students chose these groups based on personal characteristics. However, Eckert found that the formation of these groups was embedded, situated if you will, in the students' home communities and the structures of the school. The Jocks primarily came from affluent neighborhoods while the Burnouts came from working class neighborhoods. The peer structures differed between these two types of neighborhoods, which helped give rise to the Jock and Burnout groups in school. In the working class neighborhoods, parents' lack of time led to reliance on older children as caretakers and the formation of mixed-age peer groups with plenty of independence from adults. In the affluent neighborhoods, child activity and peer interactions were typically structured and supervised by parents or other adults. The peer groups that emerged were based around the structured activities, including school, and were similar in age.

As a consequence of the independent and mixed-age structure of the working-class peer groups, children from the working class neighborhoods had earlier exposure to adult-like activity such as mixed-age relationships and inappropriate behavior such as smoking. This early exposure to inappropriate behavior, combined with their sense of independence from adult authority, set working-class children at odds with the school adults at an early age. Contributing to an opposition to school was a general mistrust of societal institutions by working-class communities.1 With entry into junior high, the peer groups became more rigidly defined, and the kids who were at odds with adult authority coalesced into the Burnouts.

Children from affluent neighborhoods had more dependent and approach-oriented relationships with adults due to their structured activities and frequent placement in higher tracks in elementary school. They initially formed peer groups in opposition to the "rowdy" and rebellious Burnouts and emerged as the Jocks in junior high. In addition, many gained prestige through athletic success and teacher approval, further contributing to the Jocks holding a pro-school group identity.

The pro- and counter-school identities of the Jocks and Burnouts, respectively, became further polarized over time. Burnouts often became banned from school activities for illicit behavior, leading to greater resistance. Eckert explained, "As they became excluded from school activities, Burnouts moved from being simply 'rowdy' to adopting a counter-school ideology. Whereas at first being rowdy had been 'cool,' now participating in school activities was 'not cool'" (p. 88). In contrast, the Jocks were becoming more profoundly integrated in the school structure and culture:

> Whereas as seventh graders the cohort were mere consumers of school activities, when they reached ninth grade the opportunities for active production of these activities increased. Not only were they more apt to play starring roles on athletic and cheerleading teams, but they could also work on such things as yearbook…At this point, the Jocks' image as "goody-goodies" and "teacher's pets" was transformed into a more cooperative, equal relation with staff. (p. 89–90).

Even in high school, when the social groups became less rigid and many of the Jocks began to engage in the illicit behavior of the Burnouts, pro- and counter-school attitudes persisted among Jocks and Burnouts. Thus, the students' continued engagement (or lack thereof) with school, and consequently their learning, was embedded in their social groups, which were situated in their local commu-

---

[1] A New Yorker cartoon depicted a large fish eating a medium fish eating a small fish. The small fish is thinking "There is no justice in the world," the medium fish is thinking "There is some justice in the world," and the big fish is thinking, "The world is just." Those benefitting less from society tend to view societal institutions, including school, as less just and beneficial (Ogbu, 1974).

nities. To understand the students' learning, you needed to understand the larger context in which they operated.

Context In the Forefront

On a final note, situative research can also be described as research that puts context in the forefront. In most research on learning, the individual learner is the figure and context is the ground. Situative research often switches this relationship. Going back to our animals, when we ask the question, "How is the panda adapted to its environment?" we make the panda the figure and its environment the ground. But we could flip that around by asking, "What kind of animal adaptations does a bamboo forest afford?" Similarly, we can ask, "What kind of learning does a particular educational setting afford?" And this is precisely the kind of question many situative scholars investigate. For example, Nolen (2007) studied how school contexts afforded particular kinds of engagement with writing and opportunities (or not) to develop identities as writers.

IMPLICATIONS

Instead of focusing exclusively on the situative perspective, I discuss implications of both the learning as cockroach and learning as panda bear perspectives. These two perspectives lead to two contrasting (but not incompatible) approaches to dealing with the challenge of getting students to apply learning in meaningful, real-world contexts: *engineer cockroach-like knowledge* versus *align contexts*. Then I address another implication stemming from the situative perspective, which is simply *pay attention to the whole context*.

Engineer Cockroaches

The cognitive perspective recognized the problem of students being unable to apply learning to novel tasks or new situations, particularly real-world situations. This problem is formally referred to as a *transfer* problem and examples of transfer failure are abundant. One of my favorites comes from a study (cited in Reusser, 2000) in which first- and second-grade students tackled this math problem: "There are 26 sheep and 10 goats on a ship. How old is the captain?" Seventy-five percent of the students answered 36, thus confirming that they knew math algorithms but had little understanding of how to apply them meaningfully beyond the simple math tasks they experienced in school. As another example, the 11-year-old daughter of a colleague once asked, "Do two one-quarters make two fourths? I know it does in math, but what about in cooking?" (Pugh & Bergin, 2005, p. 16).

Because of cognitive scholars' assumption that knowledge can and should be like a cockroach, they began researching how knowledge in the mind could be structured in such a way that it was highly adaptive. That is, they set about the task of identifying what makes knowledge more cockroach-like and how such knowledge could be engineered. They came up with many answers; more than

I can address here. Instead, I will focus on one theory that emerged, Cognitive Flexibility Theory (CFT) (Spiro, Feltovich, Jacobson, & Coulson, 1991; Spiro, Collins, Thota, & Feltovich, 2003) because I think it captures the essence of engineering adaptive knowledge. Plus, it is based on some good metaphors.

The basic assumption of CFT is that transfer relies on situation-specific knowledge assembly instead of pre-packaged schemas. If you only know how to bake a cake using pre-packaged cake mixes, then you are limited to baking cakes like those in the packages. If the situation calls for something different, too bad. But if you know how to bake a cake from scratch…well then, now you are a much more flexible chef and can adapt your baking to the situation at hand.

The same principle applies to learning. Pre-packaged schemas are ready-made solutions to problems. The algorithms we learn in math (e.g., cross-multiply and divide), the heuristics we learn in social studies (e.g., conflict is caused by competition for limited resources), and the models we learning in science (e.g., colliding plates cause mountains) are typically pre-packaged schemas. Such schemas help us solve school problems, but they are often too simplistic or not a perfect match for solving real-world problems. To solve real-world problems, we need to cook up solutions from scratch. This is what Spiro et al. (1991) mean by situation-specific knowledge assembly—an ability to flexibly draw on the knowledge needed to solve a problem in a specific situation.

Situation-specific knowledge assembly requires that we avoid teaching a single ready-made solution and instead build redundant and flexible knowledge networks. CFT provides a model (Random Access Instruction) for engineering such networks based on the metaphor of *crisscrossing the landscape* (Spiro, Feltovich, Jacobson, & Coulson, 1992). Suppose you move to a new town. Pre-packaged schemas, such as precise directions (e.g., go south on Boise, take a right on 34…), will help you complete specific tasks, such as finding the local fly shop. But eventually you want to develop a flexible mental map of the town that can be assembled in different ways. How do you do this?

Well, you "crisscross" the area by going through it from many different directions for different purposes and using different modes of transportation. You also use maps for an aerial representation and to identify patterns in the layout (e.g., the roads in this part of town are all named after Colorado peaks). This same principle of crisscrossing applies to developing a flexible knowledge structure. We can crisscross a topic by revisiting it from different perspectives, approaching it from different purposes, referencing it with multiple examples, and understanding it with multiple representations and metaphors. The key here is the multiple passes through the content instead of relying on a single perspective, example, or representation.

For example, I had a graduate student (a practicing high school teacher) who decided to apply this principle as part of a course project. She revised her civil war unit by assigning demographic characteristics to each student (e.g., a white slave owner in the South, a free black in the North, a teenager in a frontier town in the West). Then she had students research and present their unique perspective on each event discussed in class. Thus, the students revisited each major event of the civil war from multiple perspectives, resulting in a far more flexible understanding.

CFT articulates a number of approaches to crisscrossing the landscape. Here I will mention just one: building flexible networks through crosscutting themes. Crosscutting themes are themes that apply across multiple topics, case studies, or examples. For example, Spiro and colleagues (Spiro, Coulson, Feltovich, & Anderson, 1988; Spiro & Jehng, 1990) designed hypertext environments that allowed individuals to revisit scenes from the movie *Citizen Kane* from multiple thematic perspectives (e.g., "Wealth Corrupts," "Hollow, Soulless Man") or to medical cases from the perspective of multiple biomedical science concepts.

I use this approach in teaching learning theories. I have my students revisit each learning theory from the perspective of crosscutting themes such as the role of prior knowledge, the role of social or cultural factors, and the active role of the individual. In addition, I have them compare and contrast the theories in terms of these crosscutting themes. This provides for a more flexible knowledge structure than if I just gave them a pre-packed answer to, for instance, the question of how prior knowledge affects learning. I like to think I am making cockroaches out of my students. Not sure if they appreciate that thought.

Align Contexts

The situative perspective took a different approach to the transfer problem. Instead of focusing on knowledge structures in the individual, it focused on contexts. Back to the panda bear. What do we do if want the panda to move across environments—say, go from a captive environment to life in the wild? Well, the solution is to make the captive environment as similar as possible to the wild environment. In fact, panda researchers have gone to great extremes to accomplish this. In China's Wolong Panda reserve, they even dress up in panda suits whenever they interact with young pandas to keep the environment more authentic (Wright & Yiu, 2011). I think kids everywhere are lining up for a job as a panda-suited playmate for baby pandas.

If we view learning as panda-like, situated in a particular context, then transfer approaches naturally focus on the context. In particular, such approaches often focus on aligning learning contexts with desired transfer contexts, much the way panda researchers align captive environments with the real-world environment.

Take soccer as an example. Although there may be cognitive load issues (see chapter 3) for a novice learning to dribble the ball and make sense of the rules while playing a real game of soccer, it is hard to imagine how anyone would learn to play a real game of soccer without practicing in authentic, game-like situations. Even a steady diet of worked examples (e.g., step-by-step examples of how to run a give-and-go) is unlikely to prepare individuals for the complexities and uncertainties of playing the game.

This principle of learning in an authentic context applies to school learning as well. Decontextualized learning of knowledge and skills (e.g., doing math facts drills apart from any real-world context) and studying worked examples serve a valuable purpose. But direct instruction only goes so far. If we want students to apply such knowledge and skills, we also need to identify real-world application contexts, align learning environments to these contexts, and give students learning experiences in these environments. Too often we fail to do this. I like to joke that if we taught kids soccer the way we teach them math, science, or social studies, we would drill them on the skills, quiz them on the history of soccer, and lecture endlessly about the rules without ever having them play an actual game of soccer.

So what does an aligned context look like? One example is the Computer-Supported Intentional Learning Environment (CSILE)2 developed by Scardamalia and Bereiter (1994). It was designed "to replace classroom-bred discourse patterns with those having more immediate and natural extensions to the real world, patterns whereby ideas are conceived, responded to, reframed, and set in historical context" (Scardamalia & Bereiter, 1994, p. 266). In a classroom, discourse is often one-directional with teachers being the conveyers of knowledge and students the consumers. In the real-world, there are many knowledge-building communities in which all the participants are both producers and consumers of knowledge. They all take an active role in contributing ideas, critiquing ideas, reframing ideas, and so on. CSILE was created to align with this type of knowledge-building community and was modeled after key characteristics of the academic publishing process within scientific communities. It has been used in classrooms from elementary school to college.

CSILE is a computer environment that puts a community database at the center of classroom activity. Students author this database by creating text or graphical notes, commenting on other students' notes, and organizing notes into larger structures. Features are built into the notes that prompt students to identify the intention of their notes (e.g., pose a theory, provide support for a theory, and raise a question). Authors of notes can revise them in response to feedback, and they can mark a note as a candidate for publication. If a note is approved by peer review, it gets designated in the database as "published." When seeking information, students can limit a database search to just published notes if they so choose.

For example, imagine a sixth-grade class studying astronomy and using CSILE to build knowledge. A student composes a note initiating a new conversation. In a "Problem" field, the student writes, "Why is most of the universe missing?" Then from a dropdown menu, the student selects "Theory Building" and clicks "I need to understand." In the note space, the student explains that, when watching the Discovery Channel, he heard a scientist claim that most of the universe is missing, and he wants to know how this is possible. Intrigued by this question, other students post their own notes in response. Some students use the dropdown

---

[2] The current iteration of the software is Knowledge Forum (http://www.knowledgeforum.com).

menu to select "Opinion" and say things like "I think the Discovery Channel likes to be dramatic and it's probably not true" and "He probably meant that we can't see most of the universe." Other students use the "Theory Building: New information" option to add additional details about the Discovery Channel program. Eventually, a student proposes a theory using the "Theory Building: My theory" option and states that she believes the scientist meant most of the universe was missing because most of it is dark matter and dark energy. This note leads to many "I need to understand" notes with questions about dark matter and dark energy and whether dark energy is the same as the dark side of the force. Over time, many "New information," "I need to understand," and "My theory" notes appear in which the students discuss what dark matter and energy might be and why scientists think they exist. Some notes are peer-reviewed and given "published" status. Some are organized in a graphic organizer. And so it goes.

CSILE is not exactly like real-world learning communities, but it does not have to be. For transfer, it is only necessary for key features to stay the same across contexts (Greeno, 1997). In this case, key features are such characteristics as writing for communication, posing genuine questions, revising ideas, peer review, synthesizing answers from multiple contributions, distinguishing valid from invalid information, and so on. By learning in this type of context, students will have an easier time transferring their learning, writing, and communication skills to real-world knowledge building communities such as scientific communities, online learning communities, business research offices, or even religious text study groups.

Pay Attention to the Whole Context

This implication is fairly obvious and does not require much elaboration, but it is worth highlighting. Too often we focus on individuals instead of contexts. For example, we focus attention on understanding and nurturing individual students instead of understanding and nurturing a learning community. Or we attribute learning and motivation characteristics to individuals without considering the multiple layers of context within which those individuals are functioning. In fact, we so often ignore context and blame others for actions (particularly socially unacceptable actions) that psychologists refer to this as the Fundamental Attribution Error. Unsurprisingly, when it comes to our own socially unacceptable actions, we always blame the context. We would do well to flip this tendency around by taking responsibility for our own actions and considering the context in which others are functioning. Particularly as educators, we need to understand the context of our schools and our students' peer groups and communities. For example, understanding the nature of the Burnouts and how school structures contribute to the counter-school culture of the Burnouts gives educators a place to start in seeking to engage students from the working class communities that Eckert (1989) studied.

REFERENCES

Brown, J. S., Collins, A., & Duguid, P. (1989). Situated cognition and the culture of learning. *Educational Researcher, 18*(1), 32–42. doi:10.3102/0013189X018001032

Eckert, P. (1989). *Jocks and burnouts: Social categories and identity in high school.* New York, NY: Teachers College Press.

Greeno, J. G. (1997). On claims that answer the wrong questions. *Educational Researcher, 26*(1), 5–17. doi: 10.3102/0013189X026001005

Greeno, J. G., Collins, A., & Resnick, L. B. (1996). Cognition and learning. In D. C. Berliner & R. C. Calfee (Eds.), *Handbook of educational psychology* (pp. 15–46). New York, NY: Macmillan.

Lave, J., Murtaugh, M., & de la Rocha, O. (1984). The dialectic of arithmetic in grocery shopping. In B. Rogoff & J. Lave (Eds.), *Everyday cognition: Its development in social context* (pp. 67–94). Cambridge, MA: Harvard University Press.

Lave, J., & Wenger, E. (1991). *Situated learning: Legitimate peripheral participation.* Cambridge, MA: Cambridge University Press.

Nolen, S. B. (2007). The role of literate communities in the development of children's interest in writing. In P. Boscolo & S. Hidi (Eds.), *Writing and motivation* (pp. 241–255). Oxford, UK: Elsevier.

Ogbu, J. U. (1974). *The next generation: An ethnography of education in an urban neighborhood.* New York, NY: Academic Press.

Pugh, K. J., & Bergin, D. A. (2005). The effect of schooling on students' out-of-school experience. *Educational Researcher, 34*(9), 15–23. doi:10.3102/0013189X034009015

Reusser, K. (2000). Success and failure in school mathematics: Effects of instruction and school environment. *European Child & Adolescent Psychiatry, 9* (suppl. 2), 17–26. doi:10.1007/s007870070006

Rogoff, B. (1993). Children's guided participation and participatory appropriation in sociocultural activity. In R. H. Wozniak & K. W. Fischer (Eds.), *Development in context: Acting and thinking in specific environments* (pp. 121–153). Hillsdale, NJ: Erlbaum.

Scardamalia, M., & Bereiter, C. (1994). Computer support for knowledge-building communities. *The Journal of the Learning Sciences, 3*, 265–283. doi:10.1207/s15327809jls0303_3

Scribner, S. (1984). Studying working intelligence. In B. Rogoff & J. Lave (Eds.), *Everyday cognition: Its development in social context* (pp. 9–40). Cambridge, MA: Harvard University Press.

Spiro, R. J., Collins, B. P., Thota, J. J., & Feltovich, P. J. (2003). Cognitive flexibility theory: Hypermedia for complex learning, adaptive knowledge application, and experience acceleration. *Educational Technology, 43*(5), 5–10.

Spiro, R. J., Coulson, R. L., Feltovich, P. J., & Anderson, D. K. (1988). Cognitive flexibility theory: Advanced knowledge acquisition in ill-structured domains. In *Tenth annual conference of the cognitive science society* (pp. 375–383). Hillsdale, NJ: Erlbaum.

Spiro, R. J., Feltovich, P. J., Jacobson, M. J., & Coulson, R. L. (1991). Cognitive flexibility, constructivism, and hypertext: Random access instruction for advanced knowledge acquisition in ill-structured domains. *Educational Technology, 31*(5), 24–33.

Spiro, R. J., Feltovich, P. J., Jacobson, M. J., & Coulson, R. L. (1992). Cognitive flexibility, constructivism, and hypertext: Random access instruction for advanced knowledge acquisition in ill-structured domains. In T. M. Duffy & D. H. Jonassen (Eds.), *Con-*

structivism and the technology of instruction: A conversation (pp. 57–75). Hillsdale, NJ: Erlbaum.

Spiro, R. J., & Jehng, J. C. (1990). Cognitive flexibility and hypertext: Theory and technology for the nonlinear and multidimentional traversal of complex subject matter. In D. Nix & R. J. Spiro (Eds.), *Cognition, education, and multimedia: Exploring ideas in high technology* (pp. 163–205). Hillsdale, NJ: Erlbaum.

Wright, D., & Yiu, K. (2011, November 28). *Panda-monium: Chinese researchers don panda suits to study pandas*. ABC News. Retrieved from http://abcnews.go.com/blogs/technology/2011/11/panda-monium-chinese-researchers-don-panda-suits-to-study-pandas.

PART 5

THE PURPOSE OF LEARNING

Recently, my wife showed me some second grade reading test results for our daughter. Her smirk told me I was supposed to catch something about the results. Her DRA 2 reading level was listed as 14. "Students are expected to achieve levels 14–16 by the end of first grade," the report read. Hum, a bit behind. Her oral reading fluency score was 31. A score of 27–44 was labeled as "Some risk for reading difficulty." OK. Her nonsense word fluency score was 60. A score of 51 and above was labeled as "Proficient." Suddenly, I got the joke. Our daughter was proficient at nonsense! How great is that? I was very proud.

Of course, some may not think nonsense is such a worthy learning goal. That begs the question, what are worthy learning goals? Or more generally, what should be the purpose of learning? In the final section of this book, I address these questions with two additional metaphors. In the name of full disclosure, I admit to having a real bias. I am one of those nuts who thinks that the king of Bhutan got it right when he decided that Gross National Happiness (GNH) was a better indicator of his nation's well-being than Gross Domestic Product (GDP). That's right, there is a country that has a national measure of happiness and sets policy around this measure. Wouldn't it be great to have this as part of American politics? I can imagine a presidential debate:

> Moderator: Recent data suggest that GNH has declined over the last few years. Some happiness forecasters are predicting a major GNH recession over the next five years. What do you propose to do about it? Let's start with you Mr. Codswallop.
> Mr. Codswallop (Rep): I fear that the policy blunders of the current Democratic presidency will result not only in a happiness recession but a clinical depression (ha, ha, ha). Happiness, as we all know, is a

result of choice and freedom. Our great forefathers established this country as a nation of freedom so we might have the right to pursue happiness. But the current Democratic administration has sought to erode these freedoms by imposing large government programs on the American people and strapping businesses with ever more restrictive regulations. Only by limiting government's oppressive grip on America can we pull out of the happiness recession.

Mr. Malarkey (Dem): The level of happiness has actually risen during the term of the current president. Four years ago, when he first took office, happiness was in short order. The prior Republican administration, with policies favoring the rich and powerful, had created a large class division. The Republicans assumed that if we made the rich very happy, their happiness would trickle down to the poor and oppressed. This was an absurd assumption. Driving around in your new car with your new boat is not going to increase the happiness of someone driving a 20-year-old Fiat.

Mr. Codswallop (Rep): We *are* entering a happiness recession because the Democrats' green revolution has left the country feeling green. The American people do not develop lasting happiness by going to their "happy place" in the woods. They develop lasting happiness by achieving a sense of purpose and efficacy through meaningful employment, which requires that the government do a better job of supporting business growth.

Mr. Malarkey (Dem): You are wrong Mr. Codswallop. The pell-mell, life-in-the-fast lane, work 'til you drop, no maternity leave, no paid vacation mentality breeds nothing but misery. The only thing more misery inducing is war, which my Republican counterparts have proven adept at getting us into.

So maybe the debate wouldn't change. The point is, GNH shifts the perceived purpose of government from a salient, tangible goal (growing GDP) to one that is more abstract and insubstantial but maybe more true to our core values.

In education as in politics, we tend to focus on salient, tangible goals, such as the standardized tests scores used to rank schools. But are there other more important goals we should be concerned with? What should be the central purpose of education?

John Dewey, a prominent American philosopher and educator, had some thoughts on this matter that I find quite profound. In the following two chapters, I present these thoughts using two metaphors. The first, *learning as the journey versus the map*, is an adaptation of a metaphor Dewey (1902/1990) presented in a book titled *The Child and the Curriculum*. The second, *learning as art*, is the result of using Dewey's (1934/1980) writing about art (from his book *Art as Experience*) as a metaphor for his ideas on learning.

CHAPTER 9

LEARNING AS THE JOURNEY VERSUS THE MAP

The map is not the substitute for a personal experience. The map does not take the place of an actual journey ... But the map, a summary, an arranged and orderly view of previous experiences, serves as a guide to future experience; it gives direction; it facilitates control; it economizes effort, preventing useless wandering, and pointing out the paths that lead most quickly and most certainly to the desired result.

—*Dewey, 1902/1990, p. 198*

On August 13th, 1869, John Wesley Powell wrote, "We are now ready to start our way down the Great Unknown. ... We have an unknown distance yet to run; an unknown river yet to explore. What falls there are, we know not; what rocks beset the channel, we know not; what walls rise over the river, we know not. Ah, well!" (Powell, 1875, p. 80). When Powell wrote this, he was standing at the junction of the Colorado and the Little Colorado rivers. Below him waited the unexplored Grand Canyon.

Powell was a civil war veteran and geologist who became one of the great western explorers, despite losing an arm in the war. His 1869 expedition was a legendary achievement. By the time the Colorado River reaches the Grand Can-

Computers, Cockroaches, and Ecosystems: Understanding Learning through Metaphor,
pages 143–154.

yon, it is massive in volume and often runs at a furious pace through tight canyon walls over monstrous boulders. In some places, the rapids run for miles or harbor standing waves more than 20 feet high and 60 feet wide. The roar is so loud that it echoes for miles upstream, striking fear in the hearts of ordinary men. Powell was no ordinary man.

Soon after embarking from the junction with the Little Colorado, Powell and his team entered a section of the canyon where jagged black granite cliffs and spires rose vertically from the sides of the river. The river was squeezed so tightly through this section that portaging the boats or passing them through rapids attached to lines was often impossible. Powell (1875) provided this telling account of passage through one rapid:

> We find ourselves above a long, broken fall, with ledges and pinnacles of rock obstructing the river. ... There is no hesitation. We step into our boats, push off and away we go, first on smooth but swift water, then we strike a glassy wave, and ride to its top, down again into the trough, up again on a higher wave, and down and up on waves higher and still higher, until we strike one just as it curls back, and a breaker rolls over our little boat. ... The open compartment of the "Emma Dean" [Powell's boat] is filled with water, and every breaker rolls over us. Hurled back from a rock, now on this side, now on that, we are carried into an eddy, in which we struggle for a few minutes, and are then out again, the breakers still rolling over us. Our boat is unmanageable, but she cannot sink, and we drift down another hundred yards, through breakers; how, we scarcely know. (pp. 82–83; see Figure 9.1 for a sketch)

This was just the first day. It would take Powell 16 more days to make it through the canyon. But make it he did.

Upon his return, Powell published an 1875 report for the Smithsonian: *Exploration of the Colorado River of the West and its Tributaries*. With its detailed map and wealth of information on distances, directions, elevations, landmarks, rapids, and navigation strategies, it became a guide for explorers and thrill seekers for decades to come. In an introduction to the 1987 edition of the report, Wallace Stegner wrote, "Nearly everyone who runs any part of the canyons now ... either carries this story of Powell's in his duffel bag or has it read or recited to him around the fire while the tamed Colorado slips past" (Powell, 1997, p. xii).

In the fall of 2009, I had the awe-inspiring experience of rafting the Grand Canyon with my wife and father-in-law. We used an updated guidebook with topographical maps and detailed information about rapids, campsites, side canyons, sites of historical significance, and the geology and zoology of the region. The guide was even waterproof, so we kept it strapped to the top of a cooler for easy access. The thing was indispensable. It made our journey possible and greatly enriched the experience.

Such is the purpose of a guidebook. It compiles the information obtained by visionaries like John Wesley Powell and, in doing so, opens up opportunities for us ordinary folk. Guidebooks do have inherent value. Powell's *Exploration of the Colorado River of the West and its Tributaries* is fascinating to read. However, a

FIGURE 9.1.   Sketch included in *Exploration of the Colorado River of the West and Its Tributaries* (Powell, 1875).

guide, no matter how informative and interesting, is not a substitute for an individual journey. I enjoyed reading Powell's report, but floating down the Colorado through the Grand Canyon is an experience I will never forget. This is the point Dewey was making in the opening quotation. Guidebooks and maps should not substitute for personal experience, but should enable, guide, and enrich personal experience.

MAKING SENSE OF THE METAPHOR

Having the Journey

In saying maps should not substitute for personal experience and actual journeys, Dewey was talking about the role of the school curriculum and the purpose of learning. Let us lay out the parts of this metaphor. We have *explorers*, whose experiences result in the creation of a *map* or guidebook that then becomes a guide for future *journeys*. Dewey makes it clear that the map is analogous to the curriculum. So then, who are the explorers and what is the journey? In response, my students often say teachers or curriculum developers are the explorers. Their rationale is that teachers and curriculum developers "explore" the curriculum. I admit that in some ways teachers and curriculum developers are explorers, but in Dewey's metaphor, these individuals may be more representative of cartographers and guidebook writers. That is, they take information provided by explorers and put it together in a logical, more easily accessible form. So the question remains: who are the explorers? Who are the John Wesley Powells? Who are those pioneers who ventured forth into uncharted territory?

When talking about the curriculum, such territories are the knowledge domains—math, science, history, and so on. Thus, the explorers are the pioneers of these knowledge domains. The Newtons and Einsteins in science. The Shakespeares and Dostoevskys in literature. These are the people who, like John Wesley Powell, pushed the boundaries of what was known and what was possible. The knowledge and discoveries of these individuals was then summarized and made accessible in school curriculums. Their achievements became guides for future journeys in the knowledge domain. Or did they?

Dewey's concern was that the achievements of people like Newton and Einstein often become substitutes for personal journeys in the knowledge domain. That is, they become substitutes for personal experiences of *doing* that resemble the experiences of the pioneers. When I rafted the Grand Canyon, I engaged in an actual journey as John Wesley Powell did. I did not just read about and study his experience: I lived it. However, my experience was very different from his because it was guided; it built on his experience and the experience of other explorers.

Similarly, a journey in a knowledge domain involves more than reading about and studying the lives and ideas of the pioneers. A journey in the domain of science is more than studying the ideas of Newton and Einstein. It involves actually *doing* science. This does not mean that we should be forced to rediscover Newton's or Einstein's ideas (like any of us are smart enough to do that!). Rather, it means that the science ideas of the past should be learned and used as guides for having our own science experiences. But this rarely happens.

Science classes in school often focus on terminology (oh, the terminology) at the expense of actually doing science. And do not assume those labs you engaged in count as doing real science. All too often, these labs are "cookbook" labs simply requiring students to follow instructions like those of a recipe. My oldest daughter hates this. As a child, she loved science. From the ages of three to four, she thought she was the planet Saturn. Seriously, she did. She ran around all day telling stories about her adventures as Saturn with her stuffed cat Titan (yep, named after Saturn's largest moon). But in high school, she often came home with complaints like, "Science labs are a waste of time! I know what the answer is supposed to be, but I still have to go do the stuff anyway to get the right answer. Or construe the evidence to get the right answer. It's never like you have to actually *think*!"

This is not the kind of "doing" Dewey had in mind. The journey, the doing of science, is to engage in discovery and exploration. It is to use the great discoveries of the past to figure out more about how the world works. This is the journey that pioneers like Newton and Einstein valued. This is *why* they engaged in science.

Other knowledge domains also have their maps and journeys. In literature, knowledge of grammar, writing structure, and how to write a thesis statement are part of the map. Acting as an actual writer or a literary critic is the journey. In history, learning about historical events and causes of conflict is the map. Using these ideas to debate current events or do your own historical analysis of an event is the journey. In foreign language, learning the vocabulary is the map. Using this knowledge to interact with individuals from other cultures is the journey. And so on.

Earning the Fishing Merit Badge Without Fishing

Perhaps the meaning of "having the journey" versus letting the map substitute for the journey can best be illustrated through successes and failures in out-of-school learning contexts.

I have spent many years a leader in the Boy Scouts of America, and sometimes it kills me when my scouts only care about the map, not the journey. In the Boy Scouts, the map is the requirements for earning a merit badge[1]. The knowledge conveyed through these requirements should be a guide to all sorts of journeys, including personal experiences with nature, citizenship, physical fitness, and so on. But far too often, the merit badges become goals unto themselves and the journey is missed.

I once took my scouts to a local nature preserve when we were working on the Nature merit badge. As we arrived, I spotted an osprey sitting on a telephone pole with a large fish in its talons. I thought, *How perfect is this? I'm totally going to get these kids hooked on nature watching.* Unfortunately, most of the scouts got stuck on the merit badge requirements. They were consumed with questions like, *How many birds do we have to identify? Does the fish count as a fish observation if it's dead?* They missed the journey.

The requirements themselves do not always help. Take the Fishing merit badge as an example. Scouts are required to do a myriad of things such as learn first aid for everything from puncture wounds to heatstroke (yes, heatstroke), memorize all the parts of a rod and reel, tie a bunch of knots, name five kinds of bait and lures, read the fishing regulations, and so on until finally we get to requirement #9: "Catch at least one fish." You can virtually complete the Fishing merit badge WITHOUT EVER GOING FISHING! It is almost like requirement #9 was

---

[1] These are awards boys earn.

thrown in as an afterthought. Catch one fish. How are you ever going to take interest in the great journey that is fishing if you only catch one fish?

The Fly Fishing merit badge is just as bad. You even have to kill and eat the one fish, which kind of goes against the whole "catch and release" ethos surrounding fly fishing. If I were in charge, I would rewrite the requirements like this:

1. Go fly fishing.
    a. Go fly fishing in a stream.
    b. Go fly fishing in a river.
    c. Go fly fishing in a pond ~~or~~ and a lake.
    d. Go fly fishing with your grandpa.
    e. Go fly fishing with your fanatic uncle.
2. Catch, photograph, and release at least four kinds of fish. When photographing, demonstrate proper technique by holding the fish way out in front of you and near the camera so it looks bigger.
3. Learn the meaning of the following terms and use them while fishing:
    a. *LDR (Long Distance Release).* Use when the fish gets off before being netted.
    b. *Fish on the brain.* Use as an explanation for why you are late returning from fishing, lost your jacket, forgot to do you chores, etc.
    c. *Fish on.* Use when you hook a fish or as a motto for life.
    d. *Just one more cast.* Use (repeatedly) whenever it is time to go.
4. Go to a fly shop and do the following:
    a. Talk fishing stories with the owner. Demonstrate proper use of exaggeration and hyperbole when telling fishing stories.
    b. Make a list of 10 unneeded pieces of gear and why you have to have them anyway.
5. Go fly fishing some more.
6. Learn proper first aid for getting a fly out of:
    a. Your neck
    b. Your ear
    c. Your shin
    d. Your finger
    e. The tip of your nose [yes, I'm speaking from personal experience here—and I left out a few body parts].
7. Study the ecological disaster of introducing lake trout into Yellowstone Lake.

Some years back, I took my scouts backpacking in the Snowy Range in Wyoming. I figured it would be a good opportunity to work on the Fly Fishing merit badge because the area is dotted with lakes and streams full of eager trout. However, I did not want my scouts to focus on the merit badge and miss the journey, so I did not mention the requirements. I just taught the three scouts with me how to tie on a fly, gave a few casting instructions, and took them to a tiny creek.

My scouts began flailing the fly rods about, and I ducked and weaved among them giving pointers while trying to avoid being hooked. For a moment, I feared I was going to have to take a more serious approach, but then I heard, "Hey! I got one!" I looked up, and Riley was hauling an eight-inch Brook trout out of the creek. As I helped Riley unhook and release the fish, I looked back to see Bryce with a fish on, too. By the time I helped Bryce release his fish, Riley had another one. It was a good start. Riley and Bryce were having a great time. Josh, not so much.

"Arrr. I can't catch any of these dumb fish," he remarked. He was standing right next to the creek splatting his fly down at some fish cowering in the bottom of a small pool.

"Uh Josh, those fish see you." *Splat, splat.*

"They aren't going to eat your fly." *Splat, splat, splat.*

Eventually Josh gave up, and we moved to another pool. After a few errant casts and another fish by Riley, we finally got the fly to land at the head of the pool. Seconds later, a fish splashed at the fly. "Strike! Strike!" I yelled. Josh sat there. "Set the hook! Lift the rod!" I frantically gestured with my arms. Josh finally lifted the rod, but the fish was long gone. Meanwhile, Riley was yelling, "Hey guys! Look! I got another one! This is awesome!" I glanced downstream and saw Bryce releasing a fish, too. I did not mention this to Josh.

Two more fish took the fly as Josh continued casting into the pool. Two more times Josh sat there while the fish ate the fly and spit it back out, and then he jerked the rod violently backward. "I hate fly fishing," Josh muttered. *Splat, splat, splat* went a bunch more casts into the pool. "Let's move up," I recommended.

I leapfrogged Josh ahead of Riley and set him up on beautiful little run. After a few casts into the bushes and grass, Josh got the fly on the water floating through the run. "Strike! Strike! Strike!" I yelled as a fish darted up and ate the fly. Josh struck. "Alright! Fish on!" Then it wasn't. "Oh! LDR[2]!"

"Arrr! This is so dumb!" exclaimed Josh at the same Riley yelled, "Look at this one! It's so bright! This is awesome! Fly fishing rules!"

We continued to work our way up the stream. Josh LDRed another fish or two. Finally, a tiny fish came and ate Josh's fly. Josh jerked the rod violently. *Swish splop* went the little fish as it sailed by my head and landed in a snow bank about twenty feet away.

"You got it!" I cried. Josh finally smiled.

Josh caught a few more as we fished our way up to where the creek came out of a lake. Then, after retrieving the rain jackets and water bottles the boys had set down and forgotten (fish on the brain), we hiked cross-country to a meadow with another creek running through it. There we ate lunch, sat out a brief thunderstorm, and began fishing our way back up to camp. Josh was definitely doing better. At a

---

[2] As you may or may not recall from my proposed list of Fly Fishing merit badge requirements, LDR stands for *Long Distance Release.*

sharp bend in the creek, Josh hooked a fish that darted madly around the hole until we finally got it into a side eddy and scooped it up. It was a monster!—at least for this tiny creek. The biggest fish we had caught all day. "Awesome!" declared an ecstatic Josh. "Fly fishing is the *best!*"

A little later, I sat watching a black mass of storm clouds heading our direction. I told the boys it was time to go back to camp. Riley and Bryce had each caught over 30 fish by this point. Josh had caught about 10 and was still beaming about his big one. After some complaining, they all agreed to head back to camp until Bryce realized he was missing his tackle box (fish on the brain). Josh remembered seeing it at the lunch spot and volunteered to go back and get it with Bryce.

"All right," I responded. "You both have your rain jackets, right? [Yep] And you know how to get back to camp? [Yep] Just keep following this creek back to where we started. You'll recognize that place, right? [Yep] All right. You know what to do if you get caught in a lightning storm, right? [Yep] Ok. We'll meet you back at camp."

Some time later I was sitting in my tent with the other adult leader as a furious lightning and hailstorm raged outside thinking, *Where are those guys? They should have been back by now! They should have been back 20 minutes ago. I knew I shouldn't have sent them off alone. I'm the worst Scoutmaster ever.* Each time the lightning struck in a blinding flash and the thunder boomed like a cannon going off, I would get a jolt of anxiety and picture my boys taking shelter under a huge tree just as it got hit by lightning. *No, they're not that dumb*, I told to myself. *I taught them a million times not to take shelter under a tree in a lightning storm.* After another 10 minutes or so, I finally turned to my partner and said, "I better go look for those guys." I slipped on my raingear and walked out into the storm. It did not take long to hit the junction of the trail and the creek, and there I found a bedraggled Bryce and Josh walking up the hill.

"That was craaaazy," Bryce commented as I approached them. "Lightning was like everywhere and the hail was freezing and it *hurt*."

"You didn't sit under a big tree, did you?" I asked.

"No, I sat under a bush," replied Bryce, "and the hail like totally flattened it." He laughed. Then he glanced at Josh.

"You didn't sit under a tree, did you, Josh?"

Josh looked at Bryce then gave a guilty smile.

"Josh!!!"

I paused for a moment and looked at these two wet and cold boys. Finally, I spoke, "You went fishing more, didn't you?"

Bryce looked at Josh. Josh looked at Bryce. Then they both broke out in guilty grins. "Yeah, we did," responded Bryce. Outwardly, I frowned. But inwardly, I smiled. They were just like me! I did the exact same thing when I was their age. These boys were not just learning about fly fishing; they were having their own personal experience. They were embarking on the journey. I was so proud.

We never did get around to completing the merit badge.

IMPLICATIONS

Don't Let the Map Substitute For the Journey

This implication is obvious and hopefully you have a sense of what this means by now, but let me give another example just to make sure.

In the fall of 1994, Erin Gruwell was a first-year teacher at Wilson High School in Long Beach, California. She was assigned to teach freshman English to "at-risk" kids—primarily black, Hispanic, and Asian kids whose lives had been thrown into disarray by poverty, drugs, abuse, and gang warfare.

After witnessing the anger, intolerance, and suffering of her students, Gruwell decided that English class would be about the journey, not the map. This decision initiated a four-year odyssey in which the students learned to use literature as a guide for transforming their own lives and neighborhoods. The key transformative moment took place their sophomore year when Gruwell challenged them to make a "toast for change" and engaged them in reading *Anne Frank: The Diary of Young Girl* and *Zlata's Diary: A Child's Life in Sarajevo*. The students identified with the hate and oppression endured by Anne Frank and Zlata and took strength from the girls' bravery. As an example, one student wrote in her diary,

> Like Anne and Zlata, I have an enemy who is gung-ho for dictatorship: my father… I've watched my mother being beaten half to death. … I can still feel the sting from the belt on my back and legs as he violently lashed me in his usual drunken state of mind. … I can relate to Anne and Zlata. Like them, I have a diary, I write about how it feels to have disgust and hatred centered directly on you because of who you are. … I guess I'll have to wait for the war to end like Anne and Zlata did, except I won't die or get taken advantage of. I'm going to be strong. (The Freedom Writers, 1999, p. 72–73)

Another student wrote a letter to Zlata stating,

> In your diary you said you watched out for snipers and gunshots. I watch out for gangsters and gunshots. Your friends died of gunshots and my friend Richard, who was fifteen, and my cousin Matthew who was nineteen, also died of gunshots. … The main reason I'm writing this letter to you, Zlata, is because I know you've been in this kind of situation. Your experience moved me and made this big football player cry. (The Freedom Writers, 1999, p. 78–79)

Due in part to the students' enthusiasm, Gruwell arranged for Meip Gies (a woman who helped shelter Anne Frank and rescued her diary) and Zlata to meet with her students. Meeting these individuals was transformative. They began to see similarities between racially motivated gang warfare and the racial cleansing that occurred in Germany and Bosnia. They were moved by the courage of both Meip and Zlata and began to believe they could demonstrate similar courage fighting against intolerance and healing from abuse. The classroom was becoming a community for change.

In their junior year, the students took another important step forward. They decided to follow in the footsteps of Anne Frank and Zlata by using personal diaries as a way of responding to their circumstances. They labeled themselves the Freedom Writers. This act initiated a new phase of the journey that ultimately resulted in a *New York Times* #1 bestselling book: *The Freedom Writer Diary: How a Teacher and 150 Teens used Writing to Change Themselves and the World around Them* (which was later adapted into a Hollywood movie). But more importantly, it resulted in changed lives for the Freedom Writers. At the beginning of their freshman year, nearly all were failing school, involved in gang violence, caught up in drugs, or emotionally damaged from abuse. By the end of their senior year, nearly all were college-bound and committed to changing the world.

Thousands of students have read Anne Frank's diary. It is one of the ten most read books in the world. But for how many was it just a book? I read it as a student. I took notes. I answered essay questions. But I never used it as a guide for having my own journey like the Freedom Writers did. I let the map substitute for the journey. How often does this happen in education? How often are books treated as just texts to be mastered rather than guides for changing our world and transformative our relationships?

You Don't Have to Throw Out the Map to Have the Journey

In Dewey's day (and ours for that matter) there were individuals who argued that imposing a curriculum on the students constrained their experience. Many argued that students would have much richer educational experiences if they are allowed to discover knowledge for themselves and not forced to learn the ideas of others. Dewey certainly valued the process of discovery, but he felt it was absurd to propose that we have to choose between discovery and the curriculum, as if these were two mutually exclusive educations (Dewey hated such "either-or" thinking, as he referred to it). According to Dewey the problem with traditional, curriculum-centered education was not that it taught pre-determined ideas. Rather, the problem was that these ideas were treated as *ends unto themselves* rather than means for enriching and expanding personal experience.

I once learned the dangers of unguided discovery learning the hard way. I was seventeen years old and went rock climbing with a friend up Bell's Canyon near Salt Lake City, Utah. We took along a guidebook, but stupidly I (a) only glanced at it and (b) left it at the bottom of the cliff. A few rope lengths up the cliff I ran into a juncture in the crack system and did not know which way to go. With no guidebook available, I did the smart thing and sent my friend on ahead. After the rope ran out (not a good sign), I did my best to communicate with my friend who was now out of sight and earshot. Some tugs on the rope seemed to confirm that he was anchored in above and I began to climb. A problem soon became obvious. There was virtually nowhere in the crack to place the gear that catches you if you fall. No gear placements, and you might as well leave your climbing rope at home.

I finally made it to my friend who was shaking and hanging by a few dicey pieces of gear. If either one of us had slipped while climbing ... well, I do not really want to think about that. After traversing sideways and repelling off a "chickenhead" (a protrusion on the rock face) and then a dead, scraggly tree, we finally made it to a gully where we could scramble to the base of the cliff. It was nearly dark by the time we made it back to the guidebook. I opened the book to the description of our route and read, "Warning. This climb is poorly protected and has gotten more than one experienced climber into some serious situations." D'oh!

The guidebook was there to direct my experience. It even had a picture showing the right way to go (we took the wrong way). But I ignored it and consequently embarked in what Dewey referred to as "useless wandering." In my defense, at least I was having the journey. However, by ignoring the guidebook, this journey was nearly my last.

In education, we can err both by ignoring the great ideas of the past and by treating these ideas as ends unto themselves. However, I do admit that occasionally I enjoy the "useless wondering." Once I talked my wife into taking a family vacation on the Caribbean island of Virgin Gorda. One end of this island is covered in giant granite boulders. Each morning before the sun came up, I would grab a lounge cushion to use as a crash pad and wander down to the beach to do some bouldering. I had no climbing guide. Instead I just wandered around and discovered new boulders to climb until the day got hot. It was great! There is something special about such unguided discovery. Sometimes I like to learn about a subject in the same sort of unguided, exploratory way. But the conditions have to be right. I think in most cases it is best to draw upon the ideas, insights, and experiences of the pioneering individuals who have gone before and use these to initiate and guide our own journeys. Just do not forget to have the journey.

Have We Lost Our Way?

Dewey's perspective raises questions about the current direction of education. In all our efforts to increase test scores and cover ever more content, have we lost or way? Have we lost sight of that which is of most worth? I fear the answer is "yes," but I leave it to you to answer this question for yourself.

REFERENCES

Dewey, J. (1980). *Art as experience.* New York, NY: Perigee Books (original work published 1934).

Dewey, J. (1990). *The school and society and the child and the curriculum.* Chicago, IL: University of Chicago Press (original work published 1902).

Freedom Writers, The. (1999). *The Freedom Writer diary: How a teacher and 150 teens used writing to change themselves and the world around them.* New York, NY: Broadway Books.

Powell, J. W. (1875). *Exploration of the Colorado River of the West and its tributaries: Explored in 1869, 1870, 1871, and 1872 under the direction of the secretary of the*

Smithsonian institution. Washington, DC: Government Printing Office. Retrieved Oct. 23, 2010 from http://www.archive.org/details/explorationcolo00goodgoog.

Powell, J. W. (1997). *Exploration of the Colorado River and its canyons.* New York, NY: Penguin Books.

CHAPTER 10

LEARNING AS ART

[Art] quickens us from the slackness of routine and enables us to forget ourselves by finding ourselves in the delight of experiencing the world about us
in its varied qualities and forms.

—Dewey, 1934/1980, p. 110

The above quote captures Dewey's view of art. As we go about our lives, we tend
to fall into routines. We may go through the motions of the day without really
thinking. We may fail to notice the commonplace scenery. We may even interact
with our loved ones in mindless ways:

"How was school?"

"Good."

"That's good."

"Yeah."

Dewey believed that the purpose of art was to shake us out of these routines and
get us to experience the world anew. He particularly emphasized the power of
art to transform our perception by leading us to see commonplace and taken-for-
granted objects, events, issues, or people in a new way.

This notion that art can reinvent the ordinary was principal to the American
pop art movement of the '60s. Artists such as Andy Warhol celebrated the ordi-

Computers, Cockroaches, and Ecosystems: Understanding Learning through Metaphor,
pages 155–172.

nary by reproducing commonplace objects and calling them art. Warhol's breakthrough came in the painting of a Coke bottle. Emile di Antonio recounts visiting Warhol's studio and viewing two Coke bottle paintings placed next to each other. One was a simple black-and-white Coke bottle. The other was an abstract expressionist Coke bottle. Di Antonio remarked, "Come on, Andy, the abstract one is a piece of shit, the other one is remarkable. It's our society, it's who we are, it's absolutely beautiful and naked and you ought to destroy the first one and show the other" (quoted in Danto, 1992, p. 139). The simple Coke bottle represented in stark reality with no frills or embellishments became an iconic Warhol piece that recently sold for $35.36 million.

Warhol's signature works became stark representations of commonplace objects such as Brillo boxes and Campbell's Soup cans, and familiar figures such as Marilyn Monroe. Art critic Arthur Danto (1992) explained that Warhol repeated these images over and over to liberate our closed-off perception of these taken-for-granted objects: "Repetition was integral to his vision, soup can after soup can, Marilyn upon Marilyn, until the familiarity dissolves and we sense the miraculousness of the commonplace" (p. 137). Danto (1992) provided his own account of how his perception of ordinary objects was transformed by the message of pop art. He wrote;

> Pop redeemed the world in an intoxicating way. I have the most vivid recollection of standing at an intersection in some American city, waiting to be picked up. There were used-car lots on two corners with swags of plastic pennants fluttering in the breeze and brash signs proclaiming unbeatable deals, crazy prices, insane bargains. There was a huge self-service gas station on a third corner, and a supermarket on the fourth, with signs in the window announcing sales of Del Monte, Cheerios, Land O Lakes butter, Long Island ducklings, Velveeta, Sealtest, Chicken of the Sea. ... I was educated to hate all this. I would found it intolerably crass and tacky when I was growing up an aesthete. ... But I thought, Good heavens. This is just remarkable! (pp. 139–140)

For Danto, pop art was transformative. It changed the way he viewed the world.[1]

Other genres of art can be similarly transformative. In college, I took a course on the history of dance (my wife was a dance major; I talked her into a fly fishing course, so fair is fair). For the course project, I wrote a paper on the relationship between dance and common life. I became interested in the dance trends that sought to celebrate everyday life and action. I even started thinking about rock climbing as dance and performed a dance based on rock climbing movement as part of the course project. Yes, I really did this. I recruited my wife and a few of her dance friends. We decked out in climbing gear and performed some modern/interpretive dance. Good criminy! The class must have thought I was insane. Thank goodness there is no video evidence.

---

[1] In *John Dewey and the Lessons of Art*, Philip Jackson (1998) provides a detailed account of Dewey's theory of aesthetic experience and its connection to the pop art movement.

The point is that forms of dance provide a lens for reconceiving everyday movement and the themes of everyday life (e.g., tension between harmony and independence). Other genres of art are similarly transformative. Shakespeare plays can teach us to re-see our own relationships in terms of conflicts between love and loyalty. Dickinson poems can transform the way we perceive sickness and dying. And so on. Art, according to Dewey, is fundamentally transformative. And so too, is education.

MAKING SENSE OF THE METAPHOR

Adding Lenses

Just as great works of art can change the way we see and experience the world, so great disciplinary ideas can transform our everyday experience. Thomas Friedman provides an illustrative example. Before he became known as a globalization guru[2], Friedman was a reporter in Beirut. He states, "journalism for me was basically a two-dimensional business. It was about politics and culture, because in the Middle East your culture pretty much defined your politics" (2000, p. 20). Over time, Friedman was given new assignments that forced him to move beyond the two dimensions of politics and culture. He had to gain knowledge of national security and financial markets. He referred to these different knowledge domains as *lenses* and explained:

> For me, adding the financial markets dimension to politics, culture and national security was like putting on a new pair of glasses and suddenly looking at the world in 4-D. I saw news stories that I would never have recognized as news stories before. I saw causal chains of events that I never could have identified before. I saw invisible hands and handcuffs impeding leaders and nations from doing things that I never imagined before. (p. 22).

Richard Feynman, the eccentric and Nobel Prize winning physicist introduced in chapter 1, considered math and science to be lenses, revealing the hidden beauty and wonders of nature. Below are two of his oft-cited quotes:

> To those who do not know mathematics it is difficult to get across a real feeling as to the beauty, the deepest beauty, of nature. ... If you want to learn about nature, to appreciate nature, it is necessary to understand the language that she speaks in. (1992, p. 58)

> I have a friend who's an artist, and he sometimes takes a view which I don't agree with. He'll hold up a flower and say, "Look how beautiful it is," and I'll agree. But then he'll say, "I, as an artist, can see how beautiful a flower is. But you, as a scientist, take it all apart and it becomes dull." I think he's kind of nutty...There are all kinds of interesting questions that come from a knowledge of science, which only adds to the excitement and mystery of a flower. It only adds. (1988, p. 11)

---

[2] He wrote such best sellers as *The World is Flat* and *The Lexus and the Olive Tree*.

For me, this is what learning is all about; uncovering the hidden stories and transforming the simple or mundane into the complex and extraordinary. There is a fascinating world out there to be revealed if only we can acquire the right lenses. I realize I may sound a bit evangelical, but I really don't care. My career has been focused on trying to understand the transformative potential of education. The next section reviews some of this work.

Transformative Experiences

"Every rock is a story waiting to read by those with the knowledge to read them," said Mark Girod to a class of fourth graders. He held a rock in his hand and slowly turned it for the students to see. Mark happened to be a colleague of mine. We were part of The Dewey Ideas Group at Michigan State University. This was a group of faculty and graduate students who sat around and talked a lot about what it meant for learning to be transformative. Occasionally, we would experiment with having our own transformative experiences (e.g., going to the Art Institute of Chicago with Deweyan scholar Philip Jackson) or fostering transformative experiences for students. Mark was engaged in the latter. Before graduate school, he taught science in both elementary and high school. He was currently volunteering for three months at a local elementary school. Mark had a particular passion for geology and possessed a real gift for infecting his students with this same passion. As Mark turned the rock and began to narrate its story, the students watched with rapt attention.

Over the next week, a number of these students would become engrossed with rocks. They would pick up rocks on the playground and study them, bring rocks to class and share their stories, or start rock collections at home. One such student was captivated by the idea that rocks contained stories that could be uncovered by examining such things as crystal size, color pattern, and shape. She started a "rock book" at home and often brought rocks in to class. During an interview, she explained, "I think about rocks differently than I did before. Now when I don't have anything to do, I look at a rock and try to tell its story. I think about where it came from, where it formed, where it's been, what its name is. … I used to skip rocks down at the lake but now I can't bear to throw away all those stories!" (Girod & Wong, 2002, p. 211–212). How great is that? Her perception of rocks was so transformed that she now found it more exciting to hold on to the story than skip the rock across the lake.

I also volunteered in schools as a graduate student and experimented with fostering transformative experiences. I fondly remember a student in the seventh grade science class where I was teaching physics. He was enthusiastic about learning physics in class and soon came to see his everyday world through the lens of Newton's Laws. My favorite example is his account of watching his young niece slide on the kitchen floor. He explained that this event, "made me think of inertia because she's running and running and running and she tries to stop and she just keeps going until the door, until the door acts on her" (Pugh, 2002, p. 189). This comment still cracks me up. I love how he said "the door acts on her" rather than saying she crashed into the door. I can picture him sitting there, watching this collision unfold, and thinking, "Hey, that's inertia! That's Newton's First Law in action; an object in motion will continue in motion until acted upon by another object. Cool!" Meanwhile, the niece is sprawled out on the floor wondering why her uncle is staring at her with a look of enlightenment on his face.

This student developed an interest in Newton's Laws because he considered them a useful lens for viewing the world. In an interview, he said,

> [Newton's Laws are worthwhile] not just because I want to get a passing grade and go into eighth, but because it's telling me that I can look at, like, when two cars crash into each other, I can look at that in a different way, and when I watch a movie I can look at that in a different way. Now I'm going to see things that I'm used to seeing in a different way. [I: Has this happened for you?] Yeah, it really has. (p. 189)

Recently, I collaborated with a science teacher at my kids' middle school. This was fun. I got to help a teacher plan transformative lessons, but I did not have to be in charge of the crazy middle schoolers (I think there is special place in heaven reserved for middle-school teachers). I also got to interview the kids and see the quirky ways they used science concepts as lenses for perceiving and thinking about the world. I like this student who was contemplating how to use principles of heat transfer to torment his sister:

> I do think about conduction and convection [in my everyday life]. Yesterday my sister took a really long shower, and while she was taking her shower I was thinking to myself about how I could get into the heater and block the pipes so that that conduction couldn't heat up the water, so all of a sudden it would be an icy cold shower. (Pugh, Bergstrom & Bryden, under review, p. 30)

Gotta love middle school students.

Some students made comments suggested the science class was actually making a difference in their lives (I always worry it's not). For example, one student provided this explanation of how learning about air pressure changed the way he looks at maps and thinks about wind:

> My dad goes wind surfing and he is starting to teach me too and I used to think that the weather reports would say it's going to be windy so we just go off of that. But now if they showed me a weather map where there is the high pressure and low pressure…you can actually see where the wind is gonna be blowing, you can tell that. So I think that's really cool…now I understand how it blows and why, so that's definitely a big change. (Pugh et al., under review, p. 31)

This student's life was not transformed in the same way or to the same degree as the Freedom Writers, but it *was* transformed. The science ideas allowed him to think about a meaningful part of his world in a new and "really cool" way. A number of students, likewise, found it interesting or cool to be able to explain the weather they experienced. One student said:

> There's so much put into it … there's so many different things that need to happen and I never really thought of it before … it definitely is more interesting cause now I really know what wind is, really know what makes my ears pop when I go up in the mountains and what affects it, and how it, like, affects wind and how it … well, it just makes it more interesting. (Pugh et al., under review, p. 32)

Another student said, "It's kind of cool to know, you know? It's cool to know how weather works…a couple years ago, I had no idea what the weather guy was saying…But now I know what he means by like a front, and the kind of things like that" (Pugh et al., under review, p. 32). Still another commented, "Now that I notice it, it's like cool, I totally know how this is working! And I can tell you why it's working, and you probably won't understand it, but I could!" (Pugh et al., under review, p. 33) I love the attitude of this last student. She sees her knowledge as a key that unlocks a secret world. She has access because she has the key. You and I do not.

For a few students, the change in perception is so pervasive that they think about the science ideas all the time. One of these students explained, "I think about weather all the time, like I said, I can't get it out of my head. I can't help but think about it. And when I see a lot of things it just affects me cause I can't get it out of my head" (Pugh et al., under review, p. 33).

Sadly, the examples I provided above tend to be the exception rather than the rule. For most students in most classes, learning is not transformative. Some never learn the concepts deeply enough to be able to employ them as a lens for viewing the world. Others acquire the lenses but never put them on outside of class. Perhaps they do not see the point, or it may simply never occur to them to wear the lenses outside the classroom. I like to joke that the Las Vegas slogan *What Happens Here Stays Here* applies all too well to the classroom.

IMPLICATIONS

Just as there is not one right answer to making great art, I do not think there is one right answer to making learning transformative. Nevertheless, there are some principles we can draw on and I share them here.

Surrender Is Necessary for Transformation

Normally we think of surrender as a bad thing, and it is certainly not a quality we advocate for students. When have you heard an educator say, "We need students who are motivated, committed, determined and … good at surrendering"? Yeah, I didn't think so. However, a colleague and friend, David Wong, argues convincingly that surrender is necessary for transformation.

To make sense of his argument, let's talk about movie watching. I love my two oldest daughters, but they are terrible movie-watching companions. All they do is make fun of the movie (ok, I'm exaggerating). It is especially bad when the movie is an adaptation of a book because my daughters constantly criticize the movie for mangling the book. I can't enjoy the movie because my daughters can't suspend their critical reflection enough to surrender to the experience. And it is hard to be moved by a movie when you are constantly stepping out of the experience to critically reflect on it.

This idea of "surrendering to the experience in order to be moved" is the crux of Wong's argument, and it comes from an interpretation of Dewey's theory of aesthetics. Dewey theorized that aesthetic experience requires that we open ourselves up to the environment or "suffer" ourselves to be moved by the environment. Wong (2007) explained, "Both passion and suffering mean to experience intensely while being acted upon by the world. It is to let something happen to oneself and to bear the weight of its consequences" (p. 202). To "suffer" a movie, sporting event, or day at the beach, in the Deweyan sense of the term, is to surrender to the experience so that one is fully immersed in the experience and fully open to its consequences rather than holding the experience at arm's distance.

Csikszentmihalyi (1991) refers to this type of engagement as a *flow* experience. Interestingly, Csikszentmihalyi did not set out to investigate suffering, but its opposite: happiness. He gave people survey sheets to carry around and a pager (for the young'uns, we used to carry pagers on our belts, and they beeped and displayed a phone number when called—like a slightly less annoying form of texting). Then he would randomly page them throughout the day and ask them to fill out a survey sheet each time they were paged. On these surveys, Csikszentmihalyi asked participants to rate their current level of happiness and describe the activity they were doing.

Csikszentmihalyi found that happiness was associated with a particular type of activity and experience, one characterized by being *in flow*. He stated that one of the most universal and distinctive features of a flow experience is that "people become so involved in what they are doing that the activity becomes spontaneous, almost automatic; they stop being aware of themselves as separate from the actions they are performing" (p. 53). Such an experience involves a suspension of reflections on the self and, consequently, a transformative of the self:

> In flow a person is challenged to do her best, and must constantly improve her skills. At the time, she doesn't have the opportunity to reflect on what this means in terms of the self—if she did allow herself to become self-conscious, the experience could not have been very deep. But afterward, when the activity is over and self-consciousness has a chance to resume, the self that the person reflects upon is not the same self that existed before the experience. (pp. 65–66)

Transformation occurs during the act of surrendering to the experience; during the time when critical reflection is suspended. It is at that time we are open to being acted upon and changed by the environment.

Transformative learning experiences may require a similar surrender to the experience. In order to be moved by an educational idea, one may need to momentarily suspend critical reflection. Unfortunately, this is hard because there are many forces working to keep educational experiences at a safe distance.

One such force is concern over peer judgments. Imagine a classroom in which a teacher is trying to convey the experience of being a pioneer: to leave your home behind and travel across the plains to the great unknown. A student may be intrigued by this account, but just as he is about put himself in the place of the pioneer and fully open to the pioneer experience, he thinks, *Wait, is this cool? Am I being nerdy? What are the other kids thinking? Are they getting in to this?* Just like cynical comments at a movie, these thoughts pull the student out of the immediate experience. The subject then becomes an academic one to be held at arm's distance. The opportunity for the student to understand the pioneer perspective and, perhaps, see his own life through the lens of this perspective is lost. Consequently, the learning is not transformative.

Another force that can impede surrendering to the experience is the evaluative environment. Because students know they will be tested on their learning, some may be preoccupied with thoughts such as, *Do I need to know this? Is this going to be on the test? How will I be tested on this? Am I doing the assignment right? What does the teacher want?* Constant critical reflection on the assessment of the content makes it hard to be moved by the content.

It is as if an individual stand before a roller coaster and is so preoccupied with storing memories of the cars, the track, the turns, and the hills in order to give a report to a friend, that she never goes on the ride. She never submits to the experience of being whipped around the track. She does not realize that this is the whole point of going to the amusement park. This would never actually happen at an amusement park, but it is standard behavior at school. Students are preoccupied with storing memories of content, but do not surrender to the experience of being whipped around by a powerful idea.

Of course, fear of being whipped around by a new idea is, itself, a force that can impede surrender. As discussed in chapter 6, new ideas can be threatening, and we may respond by rejecting or reconstructing these ideas. Another natural reaction is to maintain a distance from the new ideas; we treat them as academic concepts to be acquired but not experienced. A student may be willing to develop a cognitive understanding of an idea but not be willing to suffer the consequences of using this idea as a lens for seeing and being in the world.

When we refuse to surrender to the experience and suffer an idea or learning experience to act on us, then the potential for transformative is minimized. Wong (2007) put it this way,

Dewey encourages us to reconsider the essential "goodness" of suffering, in its broadest sense. Without suffering—that is, without intense, honest interaction with the world—truly transformative learning is impossible. Without suffering, we cannot be moved and, therefore, cannot be overtaken in the experience passion. Our basic humanness depends on suffering of this kind and is diminished in its absence. (pp. 215–216)

How do we make it possible for individuals to overcome these inhibiting forces and surrender to the experience? Obviously, we cannot force this type of engagement. However, I suspect there are some ways we can create an environment where surrender is possible. One way would be to create a classroom learning community, one in which the students feel safe and share a collective value for learning. Educators such as Nel Noddings (e.g., *The Challenge to Care in Schools: An Alternative Approach to Education,* 2005) and Barbara Rogoff (e.g., Rogoff, Turkanis, & Bartlett, 2001, *Learning Together: Children and Adults in a School Community*) have written extensively about the nature of such communities.

I have a colleague who teaches a Psychology of Prejudice course. Due to the controversial material in the course, I would expect students to act defensively or withhold engagement for fear of what other students will think. However, this rarely happens because my colleague takes care to create a community of learners. He makes them feel safe by validating multiple viewpoints and making comments like, "This is my belief, it does not have to be yours." He makes sure no students are singled out and no one feels they have to speak for their whole racial, ethnic, or gender community. Debates are kept within certain bounds of respect, and students are treated as intelligent adults. In fact, he often refers to the students as "intelligent adults." Consequently, a surprising number of students are willing to surrender to the experience and deeply engage with ideas that can be uncomfortable.

A second strategy would be to place emphasis on learning as opposed to evaluation and social comparison. Motivation researchers distinguish between mastery and performance goal orientations. Students with a mastery goal orientation focus on learning and individual improvement. Students with a performance goal orientation focus on the perceptions of others (i.e., Do I look smart? Do I look dumb?) and/or performance relative to others (Ames, 1992; Dweck & Leggett, 1988)[3]. Focusing on learning as opposed to concerns about the perceptions of others is more conducive to surrendering to the experience. Indeed, my colleagues and I found that students who more strongly endorsed a mastery goal orientation also reported greater levels of transformative experience (Pugh, Linnenbrink-Garcia, Koskey, Stewart, & Manzey, 2010). These goal orientations are influenced by

---

[3] The two orientations are not mutually exclusive and researchers also distinguish between approach and avoidance orientations. For instance, students can have a performance approach orientation (I want show others I'm smart) and/or a performance avoidance orientation (I want to avoid looking dumb) (Elliot, 1997).

the environment. Teachers can create a mastery environment instead of a performance by doing such things as expressing value for the content, treating mistakes as opportunities to learn, focusing on individual improvement, emphasizing the process of learning, giving students a sense of ownership for their learning, and de-emphasizing comparative and public evaluation (Ames, 1992; Ames & Archer, 1988).

A third strategy would be for teachers to express their own passion for the content. Perhaps nothing makes us as willing to surrender to an experience as another person's passion. I had a geology professor who was very passionate about geology. He always brought slides into class of the latest feature of geological interest he had seen. For example, he would show a picture taken through an airplane window and say, "I was flying over Wyoming and I saw this incredible plunging anticline. Isn't that just amazing? I had to climb over this old lady next to me to get these pictures, but it was worth it." Or he would show a picture of a hillside that had been cut for a road and say, "My wife hates it when I always stop to take pictures of road cuts, but just look at this. How could I drive by? You can see an ancient riverbed starting right here." Then he would point at the picture with a long bamboo stick he always carried around and begin dissecting the image for us. He was like a kid discovering hidden eggs at an Easter egg hunt. His passion was contagious. I did not think about the test or worry about being a nerd because this professor was having such an exciting life. Soon I began to stop at road cuts too.

Classic Status Is Bad

Dewey (1934/1980) began his book on aesthetics by commenting on classic works of art:

> The very perfection of some of these products, the prestige they possess because of a long history of unquestioned admiration, creates conventions that get in the way of fresh insight. When an art product once attains classic status, it somehow becomes isolated from the human conditions under which it was brought into being and from the human consequences it engenders in actual life experience. (p. 3)

Dewey's point was that when art products becomes classics, we stop reflecting on the experience they came from and stop thinking about how they might relate to and inform our own personal experience in the world. He further explained that such art products lose their significance and "art is remitted to a separate realm, where it is cut off from that association with the materials and aims of every other form of human effort, undergoing, and achievement" (p. 3). The art products lose their significance because they no longer have the potential to transform everyday experience.

The same could be said of classic concepts that comprise a typical school curriculum. Such concepts also have a "long history of unquestioned admiration." So much so that their purpose and significance is simply accepted as a given. We teach Newton's Laws because we have always taught Newton's Laws. They are Newton's Laws, for heaven's sake! Unfortunately, this blind acceptance of significance is hollow because we then fail to search out the genuine significance: the contribution that the concepts make to everyday life. That is, we do not contemplate the "human consequences it engenders in actual life experience." Simply put, we do not consider what difference it makes.

Dewey states that it is the task of the art philosopher "to restore continuity between the refined and intensified forms of experience that are works of art and the everyday events, doings, and sufferings that are universally recognized to constitute experience" (p. 3). Likewise, we may say the task of the educator is to restore a continuity between refined forms of knowledge that are curricular concepts and the everyday experiences of the student. How can this be achieved? One solution may be to craft the content in a similar way that an artist crafts clay, paint, movement, or words.

Artistically Craft the Content

I took oil painting classes for a number of years in my youth. My instructor often told me to do things like alter the composition to remove clutter, use light and shadow to direct the eye, and add more details in the focal area while leaving other parts as broad strokes. But I didn't get it. I saw my task as recreating the photograph as perfectly as possible. It was not until college that I realized I was missing the whole point of art. For the most part, artists do not try to re-create reality. They try to craft reality in a way that evokes a particular experience. They are deliberate in what they select and reject, how they want the audience to experience the work, and how they present the focal object.

Take for example Raphael's *School of Athens* (1510–11), a fresco located in the Vatican (see Figure 10.1). The fresco depicts many of the great thinkers and artists from Greek times to the Renaissance. But these individuals are not simply lined up like a class photo. Instead they are spread out across a vast cathedral space. Huge vaulted ceilings rise above the figures, and the vaults extend into the far distance giving an impression of great depth and expansion of space, a space filled with an abundance of light. The building and figures are presented in near perfect symmetry along a vertical axis. Figures are arranged in circular groups and the vaults convey a set of concentric circles moving out from the center of the picture. In the center of the innermost circle stand Plato and Aristotle. Symmetric diagonal lines converge on these two figures as well, drawing our attention there. The figures are painted in a clean, smooth manner almost as if they are Greek statues. The colors used are again clean and vibrant. All of these qualities combine to create an impression. The balance, the harmony, the amplified space, the light, the classic form, the clean colors all give a sense of perfection, transcendence, and divinity. To me, is as if Raphael is saying, "We are the gods. We are touched by divinity. And Plato and Aristotle led the way."

Raphael gave considerable thought to the type of experience he wished to evoke. Me? I just painted.

FIGURE 10.1.   Raphael's *School of Athens* (1509–1511).

Sometimes I think educators teach the way I painted. Instead of thoughtfully selecting particular content and rejecting non-essential information, we teach nearly everything and, instead of crafting the chosen content in an evocative way, we just present it as content to be learned because, well, it's the classic content. Certainly, not all educators do this. I have observed teachers who are masters at crafting content, and I envy their skills. But I have also observed teachers who seem to give little thought to the artistic crafting of content. It is not that these teachers are thoughtless or bad teachers. It is simply that this idea of artistically crafting the content is not emphasized in school culture or teacher training programs.

What does the artistic crafting of content look like? This is a difficult question to answer because there is no single approach. Nevertheless, I hope to provide some insight by describing one approach that focuses on transforming concepts into ideas. The distinction between concepts and ideas is yet another Deweyan product (see *How We Think*, 1933, p. 132). For Dewey, concepts are established meanings. Ideas are possibilities, as in "Hey, I have an idea. What if…" The curriculum is comprised of concepts: the canonized knowledge of the past that has largely become commonplace and taken-for-granted (i.e., it has attained classic status). However, each of these concepts was once an idea that moved and transformed the world. As teachers, we can reanimate concepts by helping students appreciate their significance *as ideas*.

I was confronted with this task when preparing to teach Newton's Laws to the middle school students. Newton's Laws are, after all, laws. How could I get kids to appreciate and engage with them as *ideas*? I raised this question to the Dewey Ideas Group, and we debated a number of possibilities. I also researched some of the history and circumstances of Newton's Laws. I came up with was a statement something like this:

Isaac Newton came up with a few simple ideas about the movement of objects. You might think such a thing wouldn't make much of a difference. We all come up with ideas all the time. But Newton's ideas were different. His ideas came with a magnificent, but terrifying power—the power to explain, predict, and control the world to a frightening degree. Since that day, the world has never been the same. (Pugh & Girod, 2007, p. 15)

I then shared with the students some of the information on Newton's Laws provided in chapter 6. I talked about how this idea of Newton's changed the way people thought about God and His involvement in the universe. I talked about how the idea led some people to question the existence of freewill. But mainly I talked about this magnificent and terrifying power to explain, predict, and control. Science gave us unprecedented power over the world and Newton's Laws, as much as anything, ushered in the scientific age. The world truly never has been the same.

On other occasions, I told the students that Newton's Laws could change the way they saw the world. Things they never understood would suddenly make sense. Events that simply happened could now be explained. A hidden world of forces, actions, and reactions would be revealed. This is the idea, the possibility, that I wanted students to engage with: Newton's Laws might provide access to an exciting new world. I hoped that this framing of the content would get students to appreciate Newton's Laws as the profound idea that it was rather than just another curriculum classic to be learned. It certainly did for my student who was mesmerized by the idea of inertia when he watched his niece slide across the floor.

My friend Mark Girod was particularly adept at using metaphors to transform concepts into ideas. The concepts of rock classification, crystal formation, and weathering became the metaphor *every rock is a story waiting to be read*. Erosion became *a war between earth's resistive and destructive forces*. Metaphors are powerful tools for transforming concepts into ideas because they are fundamentally about possibilities. Mark's metaphors posed intriguing possibilities about the content; a rock may contain stories; erosion may be a war. These possibilities often lead students to action. One of Mark's students commented on erosion, "I see it everywhere I go now. At recess, all us girls, we normally sing and dance around the school but yesterday we went around the school looking for erosion" (Girod, 2001, p. 139). Then there was his student, mentioned previously, who couldn't "bear to throw away all those [rock] stories!"

Another way of distinguishing concepts and ideas is that ideas possess anticipation. When we have an idea, we anticipate. We think about actions. We imagine consequences. This anticipation is what leads us to act on promising ideas. *Do rocks really have stories? Could I read the story? What might it be? What if I gathered some rocks and brought them in to class? Could we tell their stories?* David Wong believes that anticipation is the key to transformative learning and that teachers should focus on fostering anticipation in connection with the content. He describes anticipation this way,

> Anticipation is embodied in readers who cannot put a book down and must keep turning the pages to learn whether an imagined possibility becomes a sensible actuality. Anticipation is the tension in the dramatic line that connects the "what if" to "what is." The excitement of sensing an opening to a possible world and the irresistible urge to move into the world best describes the motivation of a student who suddenly sits bolt upright in class and exclaims, "I have an idea! What if...."
> (Wong, 2007, p. 208)

It is important to acknowledge that not all anticipation is transformative. A student may anticipate humor or flashy science experiments without changing his or her perception of and action in the world. For learning to be transformative, the anticipation needs to be part of a content-based *idea*.

I like to show my students clips from the 1989 movie *Dead Poets Society*. In the film, Robin Williams plays Mr. Keating, an elite boarding school literature teacher. The scriptwriters did a great job of crafting dialogues and actions that evoke anticipation and frame the content as ideas to be experienced. In one scene, Mr. Keating introduces the topic of poetry in this way,

> In my class ... you will learn to savor words and language. No matter what anyone tells you, words and ideas can change the world ... I have a secret for you. Huddle up. [The class gathers around Mr. Keating and he bends down.] We don't read and write poetry because it's cute. We read and write poetry because we are members of the human race and the human race is filled with passion ... Medicine, law, business, engineering; these are noble pursuits, and necessary to sustain life. But poetry, beauty, romance, love—these are what we stay alive for. To quote from Whitman, "Oh me, oh life, of the questions of these recurring. Of the endless trains of the faithless. Of cities filled with the foolish. What good amid these, oh me, oh life?" Answer: that you are here. That life exists, and identity. That the powerful play goes on and you may contribute a verse. That the powerful play goes on and you may contribute a verse. [Dramatic pause.] What will your verse be?

How different is this than the typical approach, which is to give an advanced organizer such as: "This next unit will be on poetry. First we will study the basic elements of poetry such as rhyme and meter, then we will discuss symbolism and how to interpret poetry"?

One of my heroes is Walter Lewin, an emeritus professor at MIT. His physics lectures became a sensation at MIT and, thanks to YouTube and MIT's global classroom, around the world. In an interview for *The New York Times* (Rimer, 2007), Lewin explained that, for each lecture, he spends about 25 hours preparing, choreographing, and stripping the lecture down to its essence. In an interview for *U.S. News and World Report* (2008), he stated, "Each one of my lectures, I dry-run three times in real time. I dry-run it about ten days before I give the lecture. Then I dry-run it three or four days before I give the lecture. Then I dry-run it at 6 a.m. of the day I give the lecture. So in that sense, it is in a way, like a performance."

Lewin is an artist. He carefully considers what to select and what to reject. He choreographs the presentation of the selected elements. He reflects on the physics experience he wants to evoke in his students. He crafts the content in ways that emphasize its magnificence and its value in everyday life. He rehearses. Then he gives a performance. And what a performance it is.

Lewin often includes dramatic demonstrations in his lectures and frames these in such a way that they evoke an appreciation for the greatness of physics. The demonstrations are not just flash and entertainment. They are that, but they are more. They are manifestations of the power of seeing the world through the lens of physics.

In one lecture[4], Lewin has a 33-pound steel ball suspended from the ceiling by a cable. The ball is free to swing back and forth as a pendulum. Lewin has been teaching conservation of energy. He takes the ball with him as he walks to a side wall and states, "Now, I am such a strong believer of the conservation of mechanical energy that I am willing to put my life on the line. If I release that ball from a certain height, then that ball can never come back to a point where the height is any larger." He then places his back and head rigidly against the wall and pulls the ball toward him. The length of the cable is fashioned just right so that the ball comes to the height of his chin. He holds the ball against his chin and says, "I trust the conservation of mechanical energy one-hundred percent. … I am going to release this object and I hope I will be able to do it at zero speed, so that when it comes back, it may touch my chin but it may not crush my chin." He then asks the class to be quiet, gives a countdown, closes his eyes and releases the ball. It swings across the lecture stage and then comes back and stops just short of his chin before swinging off in the other direction. Lewin declares, "Physics works!" as he walks away from the swinging ball.

This demonstration is crafted not just to create momentary drama, but to engage students in the drama of discovering the physical laws that rule our world. The demonstration comes at the end of his lecture after he has walked the students through the relevant physics and math. He has led them along getting them to anticipate the consequences of the equations presented. The demonstration is a culmination of an unfolding experience. But it is not an ending. It is also a bridge for connecting the physics to the real world. A bridge that will change the way students see and experience the motion of objects in their everyday lives.

Lewin deliberately conveys his belief that the purpose of learning physics is to see the hidden patterns and reveal the beauty of the world. In a lecture[5] to science teachers, he said,

---

[4] Available on YouTube: [For the Allure of Physics] (2014). Lec 11: *Work, energy, and universial gravitation. 8.01 Classical mechanics, Fall 1999 (Walter Lewin).* Retrieved from https://www.youtube.com/watch?v=54VrCrWqaPU&index=12&list=PLUdYlQf0_sSsb2tNcA3gtgOt8LGH6tJbr.

[5] Available on YouTube: [Lectures by Walter Lewin] (2015). *How to make teaching come alive—Walter Lewin, June 24, 1997.* Retrieved from https://www.youtube.com/watch?v=M1t0egTZY44.

These [daily] experiences that we have, some of them, can be quite wonderful, quite exciting. When you see a rainbow, when you see a sunset, I think we would all agree that that can be very beautiful. However, there is more to it. There is more to it than this beauty that all of us can see. That is what I call the hidden beauty. It is the beauty of understanding. It is the beauty of knowledge. And it is our task—*your* task as teachers, and my task as a teacher, to get that beauty across. In fact, not only a task, it is your obligation. ... Teaching has always been one of the greatest and most satisfying experiences in my life. It is through the wonders of teaching that we can reveal the hidden beauty to our students. Knowledge does not narrow. Knowledge only adds.

To illustrate his point, Lewin gives a lecture on rainbows. In the lecture, he covers a number of physics concepts such as Snell's Law, the refractive index, and polarization. A typical physics professor may lecture on these concepts and then mention rainbows as an application example. But Lewin crafts his whole lecture around the idea of seeing the hidden beauty in a rainbow. *It is not a lecture on physics that applies to rainbows. It is a lecture on the beauty of rainbows that relies on the revelatory power of physics.* That's the difference. That's what makes him great.

How does he craft it in this way? One answer is that he frames the lecture in terms of the power of physics to transform everyday perception. He starts by saying something along the lines of, "All of you have looked at rainbows, but very few of you have ever seen one. Seeing is different than looking. Today we are going to see a rainbow. Your life will never be the same. Because of your knowledge, you will be able to see way more than just the beauty of the bows that everyone else can see" (Rimer, 2007). I love that statement. It is as if he hired the scriptwriters from *Dead Poets Society*. In reality, they are his own words. He took time to carefully craft them so that in a few short sentences he could foster anticipation and focus students on the lecture's transformative potential.

Lewin then goes through the physics needed to truly see the beauty of a rainbow, all the while commenting on how marvelous the physics is. He builds the lecture toward the climax in which he shows slides of rainbows and literally teaches us to re-see the rainbow. Lewin does this by highlighting characteristics of rainbows that we probably never noticed before (Did you know there is a bright cone of light in the center and a dark cone on the outside? Did you know the colors are reversed in the secondary bow from the primary bow?) and revealing the physics behind these characteristics. What is remarkable is that the physics explanations are now obvious. They do not come as a surprise but as a consummation of anticipation. Lewin has led us to expect to see certain things in rainbows, and now we are seeing them and understanding why. Just as a great writer leads you to a climatic revealing of events, so Lewin leads you to a revealing of the wonders of the everyday world.

He then closes the lecture on rainbows by orienting the students once again toward their real-world experience. He comments,

Now the next time that you see a rainbow, it will look very differently to you. I predict that you will check to see if the red indeed is on the outside. It's a disease [students laugh]. ... And all this joy and fun, you will get over and above the everlasting beauty of the bows and you will see much more than people who do not have this knowledge and whose experience is therefore necessarily rather shallow. Your knowledge adds, it never, ever subtracts.

Lewin's comments are strikingly similar to those of Feynman ("There are all kinds of interesting questions that come from a knowledge of science, which only adds to the excitement and mystery of a flower. It only adds"). In fact, many leading scientists have expressed similar viewpoints. World-renowned biologist Richard Dawkins, once wrote, "I can think of very few science books I've read that I've called useful. What they've been is wonderful. They've actually made me feel that the world around me is a much fuller, much more wonderful, much more awesome place than I ever realized it was" (Dawkins, 1998, p. 37).

Great scientists like Feynman and Dawkins pursued careers in science because they were fascinated by the way science reveals the hidden wonders and beauties of the world. Great teachers like Walter Lewin are able to craft lessons—even in large-scale lecture classes—in ways that pass this fascination on to their students. Lewin receives thousands of letters from individuals commenting on the impact of his lectures. One individual wrote, "I walk with a new spring in my step and I look at life through physics-colored eyes." Another wrote, "He made me SEE... and it has changed my life for the better!!" (Rimer, 2007).

Such comments remind me of Friedman's comments about putting on new lens and seeing news stories and causal chains of events that were never noticed before. And once again, I am convinced that this is what learning is all about. It is not about test scores and amassing stores of knowledge that largely remain inert. It is about seeing and experiencing the world in exciting new ways. At least that is what I think it is about.

REFERENCES

Ames, C. (1992). Classrooms: Goals, structures, and student motivation. *Journal of Educational Psychology, 84*, 261–271.

Ames, C., & Archer, J. (1988). Achievement goals in the classroom: Students' learning strategies and motivation processes. *Journal of Educational Psychology, 80*, 260–267.

Csikszentmihalyi, M. (1991). *Flow: The psychology of optimal experience*. New York: Harper Perennial.

Danto, A. C. (1992). *Beyond the Brillo Box: The visual arts in post-historical perspective.* New York, NY: Farrar, Straus and Giroux.

Dawkins, R. (1998). *Unweaving the rainbow: Science, delusion, and the appetite for wonder.* New York, NY: Teachers College Press.

Dewey, J. (1933). *How we think: A restatement of the relation of reflective thinking to the educative process.* Boston, MA: D. C. Heath and Co.

Dewey, J. (1980). *Art as experience.* New York, NY: Perigee Books (original work published 1934).

Dweck, C., & Leggett, E. (1988). A social/cognitive approach to motivation and personality. *Psychological Review, 95*, 256–273.

Elliot, A. J. (1997). Integrating the "classic" and "contemporary" approaches to achievement motivation: A hierarchical model of approach and avoidance achievement motivation. In M. L. Maehr & P. R. Pintrich (Eds.), *Advances in motivation and achievement* (pp. 143–179). Greenwich, CT: JAI Press.

Feynman, R. P. (1988). *What do you care what other people think? Further adventures of a curious character.* New York, NY: Norton.

Feynman, R. P. (1992). *The character of physical laws.* London, UK: Penguin.

Friedman, T. L. (2000). *The Lexus and the olive tree: Understanding globalization.* New York, NY: Anchor Books.

Girod, M. (2001). *Teaching 5th grade science for aesthetic understanding.* Unpublished doctoral dissertation, Michigan State University, East Lansing.

Girod, M., & Wong, D. (2002). An aesthetic (Deweyan) perspective on science learning: Case studies of three fourth graders. *Elementary School Journal, 102*, 199–224. doi:10.1086/499700

Haft, S., Witt, P. J., Thomas, T. P., & Weir, P. D. (1989). *Dead poets society.* United States: Touchstone Pictures.

Jackson, P. W. (1998). *John Dewey and the lessons of art.* New Haven, CT: Yale University Press.

Noddings, N. (2005). *The challenge to care in schools: An alternative approach to education* (2nd ed.). New York, NY: Teachers College Press.

Pugh, K. J. (2002). Teaching for transformative experiences in science: An investigation of the effectiveness of two instructional elements. *Teachers College Record, 104*, 1101–1137. doi:10.1111/1467-9620.00198

Pugh, K. J., & Girod, M. (2007). Science, art and experience: Constructing a science pedagogy from Dewey's aesthetics. Journal of Science *Teacher Education, 18*, 9–27. doi:10.1007/s10972-006-9029-0

Pugh, K. J., Linnenbrink-Garcia, L., Koskey, K. L. K., Stewart, V. C., & Manzey, C. (2010). Motivation, learning, and transformative experience: A study of deep engagement in science. *Science Education, 94*, 1–28. doi:10.1002/sce20344

Rimer, S. (2007, December 19). Academic stars hone their online stagecraft. Retrieved from http://www.nytimes.com/2007/12/19/education/19cnd-physics.html.

Rogoff, B., Turkanis, C. G., & Bartlett, L. (Eds.). (2001). *Learning together: Children and adults in a school community.* New York, NY: Oxford University Press.

U.S. News and World Report. (2008, March 26). Professor Walter Lewin, a new physics superstar [Video file]. Retrieved from http://www.youtube.com/watch?v=AaALPa7 Dwdw&feature=fvw.

Wong, D. (2007). Beyond control and rationality: Dewey, aesthetics, motivation, and educative experiences. *Teachers College Record, 109*, 192–220. doi:http://www.tcrecord.org ID Number: 12740

Made in the USA
Monee, IL
21 August 2020